RISE UP

An evolution in leadership

Matt Church

th⊙ught leaders

Published by Thought Leaders Publishing

First published 2019
This edition 2022

Thought Leaders Publishing
2B, 3-9 Kenneth Street
Manly Vale NSW 2093

ISBN: 978-0-9874708-7-4

Editing by Jenny Magee
Design & typesetting by Michael Fink

Produced for the publisher by exlibris.com.au

CONTENTS

ABOUT THE AUTHOR

Matt Church is a seeker of truth, sharing his learning through teaching and writing. As the founder of Thought Leaders and a highly respected conference presenter, he communicates, connects and challenges audiences and himself to be the best version of themselves.

Matt invites all leaders to expand their view of what is and find true inspiration. Highly intuitive, Matt experiences much of life beyond the observable and explainable. His ability to make the complex simple and the way forward clear, has him speaking all over the world. Grounding big ideas in practical perspectives, the evolution of Matt's thinking can be traced through the eleven books he has written.

Always one to draw a line in the sand, Rise Up represents the next level for Matt, as he turns inwards to understand and apply age-old wisdom to leadership.

Clear and focused, gentle and affirming. Unequivocal.

To follow Matt's unfolding thinking go to mattchurch.com
You can learn about Thought Leaders at thoughtleaders.com.au

INTRODUCTION

I almost did not write this book. Right up until I put down these first words, I was confident that I had something to share. Then a conversation rocked me to my core and stopped my momentum.

In that conversation, I came face to face with my limitations and lost the mojo to write this book. Plagued with doubt, and hitting the ceiling of my conviction, I asked, 'Who am I, with such glaring and obvious limitations, to be sharing a book such as this? Why should I be speaking to people who have, in all likelihood, mastered the lessons that I am yet to learn?

Will they call me out? Will I look silly?'

As you are reading the finished tome, the answer was yes and maybe. Yes, I should write the book, and perhaps I will look silly. But yes didn't come straight away. It was in those hours of doubt, concern and sleepless struggle that my most recent *Rise* occurred.

It takes courage to face down your limitations and accept your current capabilities for what they are. To stay engaged with the process of growth and not run back to the comfort of a previous position.

The essence of Rising Up is facing moments of truth. In these moments, you are often scared, confused or uncertain, but equally, you may be excited, energised and motivated. How you are called to a higher place doesn't matter, how you answer the call does.

Life is full of critical moments where we are presented with the chance to Rise Up, three of particular note: The first is when we choose to act in the presence of fear. It requires courage. The second is when you drop judgment and accept others for the wonderful beings that they are – regardless of how they present themselves to you. The third is when everything you do comes from love.

I offer the thoughts that follow with love, with humility and huge admiration for you who are on this journey.

I know the first moment very well; it's been my life story. I sense the second is happening to me all the time. And I know in my soul, that the third will appear when I shed the illusion of control and rest back into my inner strength, I get glimpses of this. So, I am on this path with you; I am still learning how to Rise Up.

This book, then, is from a brother to his brothers and sisters, not a father to his children. I claim no hierarchical position in this conversation, just deep humility and the selfish gain of a teacher who learns by teaching. We teach what we most need to learn and that adage could not be truer for me, than in this moment and this book.

I offer the thoughts that follow with love, with humility and huge admiration for you who are on this journey. My hope is that they help you to rise up and out; get *up* above the line and *out* of your own way.

So if you are ready, here we go!

Matt

PART ONE

1

RISING UP

There comes a moment when you decide that it's time to go to the next level, to evolve as a leader. Often this shift is more personal than it is professional. Mechanically advancing your career and business is what you have been doing your whole life. It's what you got good at, or else you would not be where you are. What's often missing in those who fail to go next level, is the deep personal inventory around *who* we are being when we lead. Starting with this chapter, this book is the beginning of that journey.

T here is something I don't often share but would like to do so, with you now. At times I feel very anxious. It is an entirely human reaction that says I can't share my ideas. That I should not speak in public and that my dreams and goals are futile. And yet, I choose to make my living as a motivational speaker.

This anxious voice is not who I am, it's not what I stand for, and it's not even my enemy. It's a voice that sometimes pretends to be me. When this voice gets an audience, I tend to want to give up and sink into anonymity.

I am not that voice, and nor are you.

Logically, the pessimistic, cynical world view that encourages hopelessness seems entirely rational. You may want to read Mark Manson's book, *Everything is F*cked*, to get a take on the darker narrative. Or you could listen to the late, great comedian George Carlin, if you want to laugh with a rational cynic. And you might grab a copy of Steve Salerno's book, *SHAM*, which unpacks the BS in the self-help and personal development industry.

Through these and many other sources, you will see that the voice is not unfounded and that it is quite reasonable. I agree with much of what these people and the voice in my head say. I like that they throw rocks at social and institutional Goliaths. My problem is that I don't believe in the premise that all is lost. It's rather too nihilistic for me. Indeed, we are rarely the voice in our heads. We are not our thoughts. This may seem ironic coming from the person who founded Thought Leaders and wrote the book, *Think*. However, this book explores a concept that is trans-rational – the idea of hope!

It is unreasonable to believe, to hope, to dream and to rise up against the status quo, but that's no reason not to do so.

Hope goes beyond logic. That's the danger of it, of course. It is often beyond reason to have hope. I think that's the point of this book. It is unreasonable to believe, to hope, to dream and to rise up against the status quo, but that's no reason not to do so.

George Bernard Shaw wrote, 'The reasonable man adapts himself to the world; the unreasonable one persists in trying to adapt the world to himself. Therefore, all progress depends on the unreasonable man.'

Throughout my life, I have found messages of hope to be symbolic moments of great personal and collective transformation. The courage to stay the path when everything around you suggests otherwise can have a super-charging effect.

Sister Joan Chittister, a Benedictine Nun, has recently written a book called *The Time is Now (A Call to Uncommon Courage)* and her message is clear. Rise Up. Stand up. Take action now, no matter if the odds are against you.

Rise Up. Stand up. Take action now, no matter if the odds are against you.

I know that pessimists are generally more accurate than optimists, but I don't care. Despite the deep anxiety I might feel, or the evidence stacked against a project or cause, I choose to live in hope. It's for this reason that I write this book. Make no mistake; I am not writing to some collective group of people. Every chapter in this book is written just for you. My intention is that there is an intimacy in the writing and perhaps in your reading if you choose.

A few years ago, I published *Amplifiers*, a 'how to' manual, designed to help leaders understand how to become merchants of hope. You can download a complimentary digital copy of *Amplifiers* at https://www.mattchurch.com/books

Rise Up is more of a 'why' manifesto, focusing on hope and optimism, less as learned behaviour and more as a courageous choice. Not as an either-or proposition, but rather an and-also one. If you want to know more about this idea, check out the book, *Learned Optimism* by Martin Seligman.

It starts with a decision to spread hope and optimism.

If this resonates with you, then it's time.

'Time for what?', you may well ask.

The truth is that you already know what I mean.

If you stop and hear these words, feel these words, you could fill in the rest of the sentence yourself. You could tell me precisely what it's time for, couldn't you? If I looked you in the eyes and gently yet insistently said, 'It's time', what would your answer be, how would you finish that sentence?

It's time for [insert your big idea].

How you answer the question 'what do you decide it's time for?' is how you get to experience the rest of your life. This question is an inflection point, a moment of truth – this moment, right here, is you being a leader. First, answer the question and then begin to lead your life in the direction of your answer. Then you will start to lead the rest of us, knowing that some will follow, and some won't. So what! Rise Up.

So, what is it that you decide to stand for? As the modern proverb says, 'If you don't stand for something, you will fall for anything.'

If I looked you in the eyes and gently yet insistently said, 'It's time', what would your answer be, how would you finish that sentence?

What positive, hopeful idea makes you choose to Rise Up?

It's time.

It is time for whatever you decide it's time for. When you stop, take stock and decide on a new direction; you are leading. The moment you rise up and take a stand for something new, something old, something different, something more, something anything – you have chosen to lead.

Every movement, every business, every leader has this moment. This leadership moment when they say *that* was then and *this* is now.

It's time.

What is it time for you to do? What do you choose to lead? I choose to lead at this precise moment; this privileged moment where leaders rise up. I choose to encourage you in this moment right now. I choose to witness the moment that you step into leadership.

It's time for you to put down what you are not and own the impact that you have on others. Remember that your past does not equal your future. The future is never real. It is only what we imagine it to be.

The rest of this book will chase some thoughts around in your head, and that's necessary, otherwise, it would be a gift card or a post on social media. It would not be this thing, this book that you hold in your hand. But whatever I say throughout this book, and however I phrase it, I am only saying one thing, Rise Up.

It's Time

Rise up, right now, and lead.

It's time.

Time for you to lead.

Time for you to help us be our best.

Time for you to be your best.

Time to put down the stories you tell yourself about why you can't.

Time to stop telling others they can't.

This is the time for that small, but powerful, feeling – hope – to take charge.

It's time for you to:

Stop playing small.

Stop hurting yourself and others.

Open your mind to new ideas and open your heart to people who are not like you.

This is not about learning something new. True leadership is not a capability, it's a state of mind. It is a moment of deep conviction where you step into a new reality.

It is time you led us.

Rise up, right now and lead us.

Remove our fear and replace it with confidence.

Replace our confusion with clarity and mobilise us all in pursuit of a better future.

Right now, in this moment, you get to choose to lead, to serve, to love, to inspire and to teach.

You don't need a course to be a leader.

You don't need a promotion to be a leader.

You don't need a team to be a leader.

You simply need to *decide* to be a leader.

Then you need to *be* a leader.

The rest, what follows now, on the other side of that decision is admin. What follows now is a life of service to others, a life of more love, more kindness, more joy and more compassion.

Leadership is a choice.

Make it.

Right now.

Rise Up.

ONLINE REFERENCES

Carlin, G. https://en.wikipedia.org/wiki/George_Carlin

Church, M. https://www.mattchurch.com/books

BOOKS MENTIONED

Chittister, J., 2019. *The Time Is Now: A Call to Uncommon Courage*. United States: Penguin Random House.

Church, M., 2013. *Amplifiers: The Power of Motivational Leadership to Inspire and Influence*. Australia: John Wiley and Sons Australia.

Church, M. & Cook, P., 2018. *Think*. Australia: Thought Leaders Publishing.

Manson, M., 2019. *Everything is F*cked*. United States: HarperCollins.

Salerno, S., 2005. *SHAM: How the Self-Help Movement Made America Helpless*. United States: Random House.

Seligman, M., 2006. *Learned Optimism: How to Change Your Mind and Your Life*. United States: Random House.

QUESTIONS

1 What do you think of starting, or changing when you hear, 'It's time!'?

_____

_____

_____

2 What is working in your world right now?

_____

_____

_____

3 What is not working in your world right now?

_____

_____

_____

4 Is there anything external you need to change in order to do more of what you want?

_____

_____

_____

5 If you could wave a magic wand right now, what would you wish for or make happen?

_____

_____

_____

ABOVE THE LINE

In every domain of life or work, you know whether you are operating above the line or not. Across multiple disciplines, schools of thought, ideologies and methodologies the idea of running above or below the line is easily understood and well documented. It takes enormous courage to decide to operate above the line when you can, where you can, and as often as you can. Courage is the tipping point on the line; you won't always get things right, but if you operate from your heart you will be OK, no matter what occurs.

We always know whether we are operating above or below it. Without needing to define it, we know where the line is, and where we stand in relation to it. It's rarely discussed, but you know the line exists. You know when you are above or below it, and you know for sure when you have crossed it.

If your partner says, 'Hey, you crossed the line with that comment,' you know you are in trouble. My kids often point to the line when I make jokes. Our version of what's funny is quite different. If I asked you 'Is your health above or below the line right now?' you would have an answer without either of us defining the line. This applies to your personal finances and your career. It spans how you parented yesterday or responded to a loved one.

My friend Michael Henderson is an anthropologist, and he wrote about this in his book, *Above the Line*. If you haven't read any of Michael's work, then you are in for a treat. His corporate anthropology work is game-changing, and his keynote presentations are extraordinary. Michael's coaching and the ideas he shared with me still resonate years later.

As leaders, we want to lead from above the line as much as possible. Acting with courage and compassion and making our leadership as loving as we can.

As individuals, we seek to live above the line as much as possible. We want to be the most caring, warm, open and inclusive people that we can be.

As leaders, we want to lead from above the line as much as possible. Acting with courage and compassion and making our leadership as loving as we can. I am a leadership expert, and despite my best efforts, I often catch myself operating below the line.

In my life, two simple barometers let me know when I am above or below the line. The first is my patience – or lack thereof – for pedestrians. You too have likely experienced the luggage-laden passenger at the airport. Stepping off the escalator and, unsure of their next move, they come to a halt, barely a metre ahead. With my face flushing and my blood pressure rising, I know I'm below the line.

My second barometer is on the road. If every driver around me is an idiot and I'm tempted to shout every time someone changes lane, then I am below the line. I try to drive in a Zen state, radiating love to all, slowing down, easing the way for all to get safely to their destination. Sometimes, though, I rage against the selfish S.O.B who races down the inside lane and cuts into a long-suffering queue of traffic. Fortunately, both these indicators happen less often nowadays.

Humility is a crucial element in Rising Up. It doesn't mean thinking less of yourself, but rather thinking of yourself less.

I opened this chapter stating that we don't need to define the line. But if you're familiar with me and my work you would know that I love models. Not diagrams, models. Mental models, frameworks for understanding. For me, in its simplest form, the line is 'courage over fear'.

My primary point of reference here is a book called *Power vs. Force* by Dr David Hawkins. He uses kinesiology, the study of body movement, to rank keywords that capture important humanitarian concepts. Through this lens, words like 'peace,' 'guilt,' 'pride,' 'understanding,' 'forgiveness,' 'anxiety' and 'despair' offer greater insight into what it means to be human and on a journey towards awareness.

While Hawkins' work may not reflect typical scientific methods, I've found it enormously useful. The words we use can give a clear sign that we're either above or below the line. Pride feels good, but by Hawkins' measure, it's below the line. Using his table of words as a guide, it becomes obvious that it's more useful to focus on gratitude, than pride. This is a practical tool, giving leaders a 'tuning fork' approach to leading above the line.

Check out Dr Hawkins' original levels of consciousness on page 16. I trust you will find his work as inspiring as I have.

Level	Log	God-view	Life-view	Emotion	Process
Enlightenment	700–1000	Self	Is	Ineffable	Pure Consciousness
Peace	600	All-being	Perfect	Bliss	Illumination
Joy	540	One	Complete	Serenity	Transfiguration
Love	500	Loving	Benign	Reverence	Revelation
Reason	400	Wise	Meaningful	Understanding	Abstraction
Acceptance	350	Merciful	Harmonious	Forgiveness	Transcendence
Willingness	310	Inspiring	Hopeful	Optimism	Intention
Neutrality	250	Enabling	Satisfactory	Trust	Release
Courage	200	Permitting	Feasible	Affirmation	Empowerment
Pride	175	Indifferent	Demanding	Scorn	Inflation
Anger	150	Vengeful	Antagonistic	Hate	Aggression
Desire	125	Denying	Disappointing	Craving	Enslavement
Fear	100	Punitive	Frightening	Anxiety	WIthdrawal
Grief	75	Disdainful	Tragic	Regret	Despondency
Apathy	50	Condemning	Hopeless	Despair	Abdication
Guilt	30	Vindictive	Evil	Blame	Destruction
Shame	20	Despising	Miserable	Humiliation	Elimination

Source: Hawkins, D.R., *Power vs. Force: The Hidden Determinants of Human Behaviour.*

Figure 1. **Dr David Hawkins' Levels of Consciousness**

In essence, leadership is about bringing out greatness in the people around you. Leadership is more about this idea than it is about vision, or strategy, or planning. Fix your attention on this one thing as a leader, and you end up with a superpower – the leadership capability to inspire rather than simply to inform. In their book, *The Extraordinary Leader*, Zenger and Folkman contend that inspiration is an ultimate leadership capability. Their framework is one of the best I have seen.

Leadership is about making sure the best version of you speaks to the best version of us. This is especially true when we are trying to create change or manage disruption. Quality leadership is you, above the line.

Many tools explore this idea of being above the line. Maslow's Hierarchy of Needs, Beck and Graves' Spiral Dynamics and Kegan's Orders of Consciousness all affirm the idea of elevating our consciousness beyond the basic survival needs of 'win at all cost, and us against the world'. Ken Wilber, the American philosopher and author of *The Integral Vision*, created a summary of the various line theory models. It lays out everything from Fowler's Levels of Faith to the chakra colours used in many healing practices. The point is that the idea of levels of awareness is everywhere. The table of words presented by Hawkins in *Power vs. Force* remains the most useful tool that I've come across.

Taking all the ideas I've learned from these sources and collating them into a concise and pure form, looks something like this:

6	Love	*Develop greatness in others*
5	Acceptance	*Replace judgement with compassion*
4	Courage	*Let go and grow*
3	Pride	*Focus on gratitude for others*
2	Anger	*Take responsibility for everything*
1	Fear	*Connect, don't withdraw*

Figure 2. **Simplified (LOC) Above The Line model**

Fear

Fear is natural. It happens for a reason and at some levels, it is biologically useful. Real fear, experienced by someone living in danger, needs to be correctly dealt with. Without a doubt, withdrawing yourself from danger is a smart strategy. Abused partners should get to a safe place. Children in danger should run.

But the fear that many experience in the safe worlds we live in is a psychological fear created by the monkey mind. The antidote to the fear we generate in our imaginations is connection. Fear lessens when you talk to someone about it. There are many great books about fear, so I will leave it to the experts to make suggestions. At the highest level, resist the urge to isolate yourself or disconnect when you recognise that your fear is being created inside your head.

Anger

Neale Donald Walsch speaks of anger as 'a wakeup call to the fact that you are not choosing the whole of your own reality.' When you are angry with others, you create walls of separation that prevent you from taking charge of your life. We get angry when we feel powerless, and while that's helpful when you need to break out of a controlling relationship, it's not sustainable. Use anger to flee, but don't allow it to become a part of who you are.

If you are not living in abject poverty or under a fascist regime but you are continuously angry at others or the world, then it's time to face up to reality. You are not at fault for your life; you are at choice. Choose again. Stop being angry that your world is not the way you want it to be. Start making decisions that move you towards what you do want. Stop blaming, shaming and proclaiming that things should be better and do something about it. Anger is the tool of the weak or the oppressed, use it for liberation but never as justification. Cowards rationalise anger to mask their weakness.

Pride

Many people are surprised to find pride below the line. To be fair, it's on the line, depending on how you define it. If your pride is possessive in any way, it's definitely below the line. If saying you are proud of someone means you are staking claim to some part of their success then yes it's pretty yuck. I agree with Larry Winget that, 'everybody's success is their own damn fault.' Many people say in conversation that I must be very proud of my kids' achievements. Pride would suggest I had something to do with it their successes, so instead, I am in awe of them. If you are overly proud of yourself, you miss the truth that you are not yet all you could be. Humility is a crucial element in Rising Up. It doesn't mean thinking less of yourself, but rather thinking of yourself less.

Brené Brown is an expert in shame and the author of *Daring Greatly*. She is my go-to person for developing courage. Brown explains the etymology of the word, 'Courage is a heart word. The root of the word courage is cor – the Latin word for heart. In one of its earliest forms, the word courage meant "To speak one's mind by telling all one's heart."'

I like to see courage as not the absence of fear but rather as action in the presence of fear. Some great acts of courage include; taking a stand for what you believe in, rejecting institutional control dynamics, calling out abuses of power, stepping into the unknown and rejecting the status quo. Follow your heart, make some tough decisions from what it tells you to do. At Thought Leaders, we stand for doing work you love, with people you like, the way you want. This takes courage, as you have to say no to the normal game most humans play and back yourself as you leap into the unknown and uncertainty of running a thought leader's practice.

Acceptance

Rising above the line involves the need to drop judgement, surrender opinions, stop thinking about others or yourself in relation to others and just let things be. There's more on this in Chapter 7 The Deadlock of Dogma, and the chapters on forgiveness. But for now, consider this. Leaders work to include people, not to exclude. It's a pretty straightforward approach that is quickly perverted by human instinct.

We all have a deep biological need to belong, and one of the quickest ways to enter a toxic tribe is to sacrifice someone who doesn't fit. William Golding explored this in the novel, *Lord of the Flies*. It is appearing yet again in the current left versus right political conversations in many countries. Blurring the lines makes people feel less safe, and as a result, they often act out against those who don't choose sides. Judging others is an act of violence and will drop you below the line very quickly. In teams, this can appear as labels, sarcasm, gossip, cynicism and jargon – all of these act to exclude in some way. Acceptance is the doorway to love.

Love

It may seem like a big jump to go from Acceptance to Love, and it is, but the steps in the ladder are not evenly spaced. Moving from Fear to Anger is a relatively short distance while going from Courage to Acceptance is much greater. So too, moving from Acceptance to Love is quite a journey. Marianne Williamson calls this the *return to love* and describes it as simple but with many steps. It is about experiences, not concepts. I will expand more on this in Chapter 3 Share the Love. Suffice to say we are all fumbling around in the dark, shining torches down a tunnel. We are all fingers pointing to the moon and that's a poor substitute for being the moon.

Summary

When you lead you to need to stay above the line as much as possible. This simple ladder gives you the chance to listen and lead from that place. Take time to check in with yourself and others around you to monitor the level you are choosing.

In its purest form, leadership is about making sure the best version of you, speaks to the best version of us.

ONLINE REFERENCES

Maslow, A.H. (1943). 'A theory of human motivation'. *Psychological Review.* 50 (4): 370–96. CiteSeerX 10.1.1.334.7586. doi:10.1037/h0054346 – via psych-classics.yorku.ca.

BOOKS MENTIONED

Brown, B., 2015. *Daring Greatly: How the Courage to Be Vulnerable Transforms the Way We Live, Love, Parent, and Lead.* United Kingdom: Penguin Books Ltd.

Golding, W., & Epstein, E. L. 1954. *Lord of the Flies: A novel.* New York: Perigee.

Hawkins, D.R., 2014. *Power vs. Force: The Hidden Determinants of Human Behaviour.* United States: Hay House Inc.

Henderson, M., 2014. *Above the Line: How to Create a Company Culture that Engages Employees, Delights Customers and Delivers Results.* Australia: John Wiley Sons Australia Ltd.

Wilber, K., 2007. *The Integral Vision.* United States: Shambhala Publications Inc.

Winget, L., 2014. *Success Is Your Own Damn Fault: The Unvarnished Truth About Business, Money, and Life.* Audible. Audiobook.

Zenger, J., & Folkman, J., *The Extraordinary Leader: Turning Good Managers into Great Leaders.* United States: McGraw-Hill Education-Europe.

QUESTIONS

1 List three domains of existence (ie health, wealth, friendships) or three roles you have in life (parent, partner, sibling)?

_____

_____

_____

2 With each domain would you say you are above or below the line of intent?

_____

_____

_____

3 Which level above the line has the greatest attraction for you right now?

_____

_____

_____

4 Which level below the line are you wanting to avoid?

_____

_____

_____

5 Armed with the awareness from the previous questions, what do you wish to do next?

_____

_____

_____

3

SHARE THE LOVE

This chapter gets straight into it. It challenges your thinking and operating model, explores five levels of world views, and unpacks how you can operationalise love at home and at work. Before you jump in and start reading, take some time to scan the different models in this chapter. That way you'll get a visual overview of where it's heading. It has three specific bus stops along the way; one is exploring world views, the next is finding deep self-love, and the third is looking at how to do and be love for those around you.

Love is an idea that sits above rational levels of consciousness. While being madly in love talks to the deeply grounded version of this idea, the higher version is to understand that love is the gateway to new levels of awareness. I think everyone has such capacity to love, but sometimes we lack the capability. What follows in this chapter is an exploration of how you access love as a leader, taking everything higher and deeper at the same time.

I once saw a bumper sticker that read *'Love is the killer app'*. Initially, I felt it wasn't that helpful. I'm not sure what I hoped a car sticker would do for me, but it got me thinking, and it turns out that thinking about love's utility at home and work, has been worthwhile.

If Love is the killer app:

How do you download it?

How do you use it?

When should it be applied?

So, what is love?

Like most questions, the answer is, it depends!

It depends on your world view and level of awareness. It depends on your luck, your good fortune and a whole bunch of beliefs and stories and so much more, that I could not fathom or share, without freaking us both out.

For a very long time, I thought it was my birthright!

It pains me to admit this, but for most of my present life, I have experienced love as something I am *entitled* to feel. As though it's owed to me – see level three on the world view model on page 27. Love is something I want, I told myself, and I will pursue it until I get it. Such an ambitious, motivated quest can be hard on those you love. Jada Pinkett Smith, in her Red Table Talks, presented a very revealing two-part episode, featuring husband Will. Check it out on Facebook. Will explains that he had a picture in his head of how life should look and that he would do whatever it took to make that picture come true. I know exactly what he means.

Over many years, relationship coach Lorna Patten, has opened me up to love and taught me how to go deeper. She has helped me

ORIENTATION	VIEW	LOVE
5 Win	*Collective*	Experienced
4 Win/Win	*Collaborative*	Shared
3 Win/Lose	*Competitive*	Entitled
2 Lose/Lose	*Victim*	Denied
1 Everything is lost	*Hopeless*	Not Felt

Figure 3. **The Five World Views**

through a few tough conversations, and one of them knocked me straight in my heart. In this meeting, a person had just explained how selfish they thought I was (they were right and wrong) and Lorna said, 'Maybe, but I see Matt as Self FULL. He has one of the biggest hearts I have ever felt. He is the very embodiment of what it means to be heartful.' That turns out to be a useful belief, and that moment permitted me to allow it into all parts of my life, to be 'heartful' at work, at home, everywhere.

You can't rise up till you have dug deep.

The Persian poet, Rumi, wrote that cracks are where God lets the light in. At that moment Lorna broke down the leader's mask I had been wearing, and called on me to be that deep love I felt inside, and to bring it out, everywhere.

The love I have been searching for my whole life wasn't outside of me after all. Crack yourself wide open to find a more profound love; one that sits quietly inside you. Your heart knows no limits, you just have to get out of your way, put down the self-harm, forgive strongly and open up to who you really are. You are heartful, and that's what gives you the buoyancy to Rise Up.

One of my mentors, Robert, sat me down and said it straight. 'Pray every day, Matt, that God shows you how to love yourself.' I was an atheist at the time and had been for 25 years. That mandate was initially about as helpful as the bumper sticker. Yet his call to me can be yours too. You can't rise up till you have dug deep.

So many books have been written on love, at every level of the above model. My favourite is a little book called *How to Love*, by Thích Nhất Hạnh, aka Master Thầy. He writes, 'A friend is one who encourages you to look deep inside yourself for the beauty and love you've been seeking.'

Master Thầy describes true love as being made up of four elements: loving-kindness, compassion, joy and equanimity. This got me thinking again about love and the idea that it is a killer app. The day I received the book, Robert Smalley sent this note to all his students. I reckon it was just for me.

Dearly Beloved,

Loving oneself cannot occur until one is sufficiently lined up with God. Obeying God's laws are part of that.

One way to get started on the path of loving oneself is to always follow this: In every and all cases be kind, caring, considerate, and compassionate. This opens the doorway to self-love.

Remember the great admonition is to love God with all your heart and soul and love your neighbor as you love yourself. This again helps open the door to self-love.

Remember you do not have love you become love.!!! This is the inner essence of God shining his light upon you. When you are filled with this inner light love automatically descends upon you and gives you that love as well as a great deal of peace.

In nearly every case forgiveness is a must on one's path to self-love. It is obvious that without forgiveness how can one possibly love themselves. So please go deep within yourself and root out everything that may be related to any unforgiveness left in your heart.

Always ask God in your prayer work to help you love yourself. I personally asked for this for many years before it happened to me. The bottom line is you will have very little love in your life until this door opens to you. Without this, one's life is generally drab and dreary and is definitely missing the key ingredient for a life connected to God.

For indeed it is truly connected to one loving oneself. I am here to assist you in any way I can.

The following guide for finding love is created with poetic licence from Robert and Master Thầy.

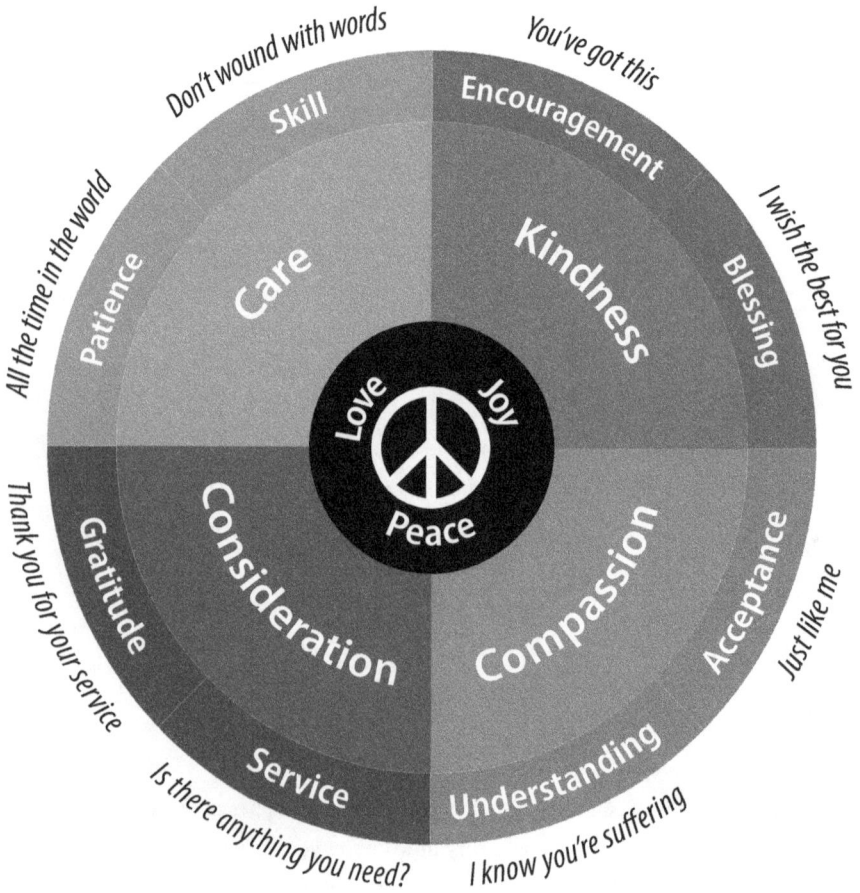

Figure 4. **Guide for Finding Love**

While the model is self-explanatory, it's also worth stating that it is clearly derivative. The fingerprints of my teachers, known and unknown, are all over this. My goal is not to pretend this is mine, as it's not. My job in this moment is to help you as leader use love as a force multiplier. I hope this model has utility and enables you to apply love everywhere.

While the model is self-explanatory, it's also worth stating that it is clearly derivative.

At the centre, your ongoing permanent focus is love, peace and joy. Possess these things they are the nouns that describe the shape of your soul. Love is a verb – a doing word, so don't ask to be loved, be loving. The practical doing of love at work and home then, is about four verbs: Kindness, Compassion, Consideration and Care. These build out into eight interpretations for how love may be applied. Think and say these eight things often and you will be sharing the love.

Kindness is the response to disappointment

Decide to be the one who encourages others rather than criticises. 'You've got this' is a great phrase, so use it as often as you can. There are plenty of haters and people with negative feedback; we don't need another one. Critics might be picture projectors, as they have a picture of how the world should be and you don't fit it. Choose to encourage instead.

Next time you find yourself disappointed in a person or situation, use that moment to practice kindness. Disappointment is a function of expectations. The ego needs to control what is and feel safe by selecting preferences, taking positions and judging others. The next time someone lets you down, respond with kindness. The goal should be to orient yourself to the flow of life, not swim against the tide. Put plans in motion, and do the work but detach from how they appear.

Compassion is the healing energy of life

Put yourself in another's shoes. See the world from their point of view, but don't get lost in it. With humility, realise that you too have been there and done that. When you see another hurting, blaming or saving, send them your love. A helpful phrase is 'just like me'. That person cut in front of me in traffic, just like you have in the past. That person is angry, just like you have been. That person is speaking from hurt, just like you have. Because you have done all these things, it's easy to see that they are you and not different or separate from you. Master Thầy teaches the power of the phrase 'Beloved, I know you are hurting, I am here for you.' He explains it in an interview with Oprah, which is saved on my YouTube channel.

Consider what is in others' best interest

We are all doing the best we can with what we have. Love asks, what can I do that is in the best interest of this person? Be polite, get out of the way. Step back, sit back and develop an 'after you' orientation. Give gifts, listen deeply, don't interrupt. The ego will scream *What about me. It isn't fair. I gave enough now I want my share.* Don't listen, it's a big baby that needs your love, but not your ear. Ask people, 'Is there anything you need?' And if people do things for you, say thank you. Gracefully get out of the way, both literally and metaphorically, and see what happens when you do.

Caring is the way to be attention out

The ego-mind has a strong self-interest. Gratitude is a tool that helps you get out of your mind's story and into what is wonderful in the world. Caring for others is a moment by moment focus that acts as an attitude of gratitude. It is one that you can hold continuously. Caring connects you to each and every person. Try in all things and in each moment to care for the souls around you. Make space, give them what they need and surrender the need to put you first. Be patient, as if you have all the time in the world and when you do speak, be loving. Don't wound with words.

Do everything with love, from love, by being love.

Maybe, just maybe, love is something you can use more of as a leader. It is certainly the way to get beyond your limitations and capabilities and discover new territory for growth.

Disclaimer

I almost did not write this piece as it's a bit exposed. I have not always shown love. If anyone has hurt me in the past, I forgive and release. If I have hurt anyone in the past, I forgive and release. If I have hurt myself in the past, I forgive and release. This mantra is the forgiveness prayer that Robert shared in my first conversation with him.

Post Script 2

I once owned an old boat; she was my Chinta Ria for 1000 days. I discovered this fantastic deck paint that sealed almost any leak. My handyman skills are not that great, so I applied that deck paint to every nook and cranny making her my Kintsugi project; bringing old back to life with love. Love is like that deck paint, apply liberally and generously, and maybe you can bring something very, very, very old back to life. Go on; I dare you to Lead with Love.

ONLINE REFERENCES

Pinkett Smit, J., https://www.facebook.com/watch/?v=2174148442809253

BOOKS MENTIONED

Nhất Hạnh, T., 2015. *How to Love*. United States: Unified Buddhist Church.

QUESTIONS

1 What world view did your parents hold?

_____

_____

_____

2 How is your world view the same or different to theirs?

_____

_____

_____

3 Can you recall a time when you held a different world view to your current?

_____

_____

_____

4 How did that affect you and your world?

_____

_____

_____

5 Do any of the eight interpretation phrases for love speak to you?

_____

_____

_____

ATTENTION OUT

This book is about two primary movements of energy: The first is the elevation implied in the title RISE UP; it's a vertical movement towards you evolving as a person who leads. The second energetic movement is out towards others. You have to go deep to get high. And when you do it's about developing an orientation towards others and a disposition to serve. For this to work we need to remove the drama that occurs in and around us, and become the authors of our lives. This chapter goes to that place. Stay open to the drama dynamics that play out in your life, and see if you can rise above them.

B elow the line is very much about you and what's happening to you, while above the line is less so. If you want to evolve faster as a leader, then get out of your own way. Get out of your head, out of your world and into the world of others.

Exploring humility is a significant first step in becoming attention out, flicking the switch between self-serving and self-referring. Humility is a word we experience in many different ways throughout our life. For many a young leader, it is a moment of deep learning – when the brashness and confidence of ambition finds a moment of discovery and realisation. This leadership moment is one to relish, to explore and grow through.

Talking about this realisation, though, is like trying to tell newly pregnant parents that their life will change. It's true, but it's also annoying. Yes, your life will never be the same, but it's annoying when it comes clad in a smug, 'I know something you don't know'. *Every* parent, if they are honest, will tell you that having a child is one of the most powerful, overwhelming, awe-inspiring experiences you can have – if you choose to see it like that.

Embracing the remarkable mathematics of our chance existence, and the deep custodial urge that is programmed into us when we see a new-born child, is truly humbling. Adopted, borrowed, bred or just met for a moment, it doesn't matter a whit when you see that little miracle made flesh.

A friend without kids said she thought she would never experience this feeling. So I asked her, 'Have you ever been in awe of nature? Simply looked at something and felt overwhelmed by a feeling of perfection, symmetry and interdependence?' I hope we all have at some point. I suggested to her that this is what it feels like to look at your kids sometimes. Kids are both *awe-some* and *awe-full* in equal doses. Just like nature.

Nature is so awe-inspiring that it's humbling. Human nature is the same.

My kids are extraordinary. I know everyone says that, but mine are. They achieve amazing feats and show unbelievable compassion and wisdom. Their achievements mean people often tell me how amazing they are, and I agree. These people also say how proud I must be, but I disagree. Pride isn't the right word, it's too possessive. Instead, as mentioned in the Above the Line chapter, I am in awe of them.

Awe is the key to humility. I did not make my kids into who they are. Their achievements are not mine. They are merely revealing themselves perfectly in every moment of their existence. Just like you and everyone you interact with. Seriously. Everyone.

Leaders understand that humility is not thinking less of yourself; instead, it's thinking of yourself less. Leadership is contemplating the needs of others before yourself while using that centre of attention to move beyond the limited, petty, selfish, paranoid, addicted, labelled self.

Three big thoughts then, at this point in the book.

1. You are not the voice in your head, you're bigger than that.

2. The best version of you is *above* not below the line.

3. Your purpose on earth is to discover who you are deep inside yourself and to appreciate the awe-inspiring vastness of your awareness.

These things cause you to drop to your knees in humility, to forgive and forget the things we and others do and instead reach deep inside to find, peace, love and joy. For you and for every one you spend time with. On the days when that doesn't happen, when the awesome is instead awful, see if you can find peace there too. I have found that sometimes we acquire more significant learnings through less desired experiences.

Knowing that the road can be easy and difficult, leaders who Rise Up understand the power of encouragement. There is a poster on my study wall, one of those 80's success type posters. It has a picture of a lighthouse and the saying, 'You can't shine a light on another's path without also illuminating your own.' Loving everything maritime I enjoy the image and the orientation of that saying. If understanding is love's other name, then encouragement is the action or access point for helping yourself and others get up above the line and attention out.

I once read that all it takes for a child's life to turn around is for one other person to believe they can. This idea is at the heart of being attention out. Humility is inherent to the act of serving others, but it's not to gain anything for yourself or from others. Zig Ziglar wrote, 'You can get everything in life you want if you will just help enough other people get what they want.' At first blush, this suggests that if you give, you will get. But it's deeper than that. You don't give to get, you give to delight, to serve, to teach and ultimately to encourage.

Books on happiness and anxiety often prescribe a gratitude list as an exercise from which we all can benefit. It's quite simple. Ask yourself, 'What am I thankful for today?' Then try to list as many as you can. While the list might start with mundane ideas like fresh water and sun on your face, over time you realise you have more to be grateful for in life than not. This orientation is both helpful and practical. Thanksgiving is an American holiday tradition, but I like to think it should be one of those universal and secular ideas that all humanity could adopt.

There are many classic sayings and lots of service undertones to this idea of being attention out. Creating a gratitude list is practical and an excellent idea, but let's go deeper. Stephen Karpman is credited with designing a concept, the drama triangle, that has become well known, written about and referenced often in psychoanalysis and counselling contexts. The only book he wrote on the topic is *A Game Free Life*. Relationship coach, Lorna Patten, introduced me to these ideas to help me get over a dysfunctional relationship with my father. It's not too big a stretch to suggest that my children got to have a grandfather because of this one idea and Lorna's work. You may find it useful in your next lift.

Humans love drama, the interplay between you and I is full of possibility for each of us to play a role. If Shakespeare is right, and all the world is a stage with us merely players, then these are the three

Persecutor
Hurts

Rescuer
Saves

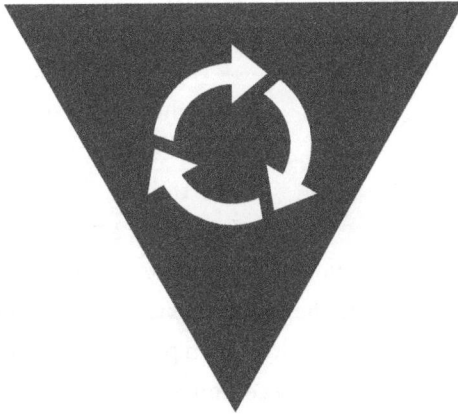

Victim
Blames

Figure 5. **Triangle of Drama**

roles most of us adopt. We are the Victim far too often; we are the Rescuer more than is healthy and, if honest, all have been or could be the Persecutor. Remove blame, hurt and disempowerment from your behaviour set. Take responsibility for being the creator of your story, instead of merely being a player in it.

Accept that while what happened to you may not be your fault, creating your future is most definitely your responsibility.

In life, there are many scenarios where these roles play out in life. An archetypal situation is in remarriage and step-parenting. Imagine a scene wherein the stepfather disciplines the stepdaughter and the mother connects compassionately to both to keep the peace. The stepdaughter sees herself as the victim of the stepfather's draconian punishment and persecution. The mother is the rescuer who comforts her and tries to explain that her new dad means well. Later that night, the stepfather is consoled by the wife commiserating that all teenagers are difficult and that this is hard on everyone. In each case, the roles between stepfather and daughter swap. In one, he is the victim and in another the persecutor.

Exhausting, don't you agree?

Persecutors are aggressive, angry and judgmental. Rescuers are over-helpful, self-sacrificing and need to be needed. Victims are downtrodden, helpless and often complain about their unmet needs. If you are hoping to get above the line and attention out, it is better to be assertive, nurturing and vulnerable.

An assertive person knows their feelings, needs and wants. They are non-judgmental and tend to frame ideas and advice as 'in my experience.' When you are compassionate and attention out, you nurture rather than rescue. You give help when asked, care and understand others; yet don't need to be needed. Finally, you know how to be open, vulnerable, realising that the stronger you get, the gentler you become.

Drama	Author
Persecutor	**Assertive**
Aggressive	*Self authoring*
Angry	*Non judgmental*
Judgmental	*Empowering*
Rescuer	**Nurturer**
Over helpful	*Give help when asked*
Self sacrificing	*Deep care and understanding*
Needs to be needed	*Not needy*
Victim	**Vulnerable**
Downtrodden	*Humble*
Helpless	*Self aware*
Unmet needs	*Open hearted*

Figure 6. **Drama – Author**

But here's the rub, we all do this, it's the human experience. Lorna taught me the power of responsibility; to understand the world as an author, not a player. I took this as; don't let the story tell you. She teaches it through what she calls the *new paradigm*, which is that you are 100% responsible for the whole of your reality. It's an idea that dances with fault and responsibility, which you will undoubtedly explore as you start to embrace the next lift. We are below the line when we blame, bully or save others. Get above the line by accepting that while what happened to you may not be your fault, creating your future is most definitely your responsibility.

If you are hoping to get above the line and attention out, it is better to be assertive, nurturing and vulnerable.

It's hard to be attention out when you are stuck in your drama. Have the courage to let go of past stories that hold you back. Author your life; thought by thought, moment by moment, one relationship at a time. Then from this place of power—your centred self—you can begin to forgive, lead, inspire, love and grow others. Shining a light on their path and illuminating your own.

You can play the human drama triangle, hurting, blaming and saving others. Or you can spend more time staying humble, giving thanks, encouraging others and being the positive, energetic centre of your world. Sometimes to Rise Up, you need to put down the stories you have of others in your life. Fall onto your knees in deep, humble surrender and focus your attention on others.

ONLINE REFERENCES

Patten, L. https://lornapatten.com

BOOKS MENTIONED

Karpman, S., 2014. *A Game Free Life - The definitive book on the Drama Triangle and Compassion Triangle by the originator and author* United States: Drama Triangle Publications.

Kegan, R., 1998. *In Over Our Heads: The Mental Demands of Modern Life* United States: Harvard University Press.

QUESTIONS

1 Have you ever been able to witness
yourself thinking thoughts?

_____

_____

_____

2 Can you be quiet enough to sense the
no-thing behind your thoughts?

_____

_____

_____

3 Studying the drama triangle can you see these in
any of your relationship dynamics with others?

_____

_____

_____

4 When you think of the Drama/Author contrast frames
(Figure 6), is there any advice you might give yourself?

_____

_____

_____

5 If you are creating all that you experience, how does
what you are experiencing right now serve you?

_____

_____

_____

LITTLE i TO BIG I

You lead best when the best version of you leads the best version of us. This requires you as a leader to take a journey through pronouns from the *insecure* self to the *superior* self, and into the *collective* self. Leadership is not about hiding you in service to others, but instead bringing it. You can't inspire greatness in others if you are coming from a place of less than. This is not about ego or identity but more about amplification. Take what is awesome in you and use it to help others find their awesome. You've got this. As you Rise Up, you become more attention out.

L ately, I finish almost every conference talk in the same way. I tell my audience that if you build your business continually considering how you can provide value to others, you are less likely to become irrelevant in human-centred leadership and a disrupted future. A customer-centric strategy *future proofs* your business and those that fail to do this don't last long. It makes complete sense. Add value for your people and your customers or clients and your business will thrive. This idea is at the heart of commerce; it's called the exchange of value.

In the world of business, they call this a customer-centred strategy. In a relationship, however, it might be touted as putting the other person first. My father used to joke that the key to a great marriage is compromise, 'Happy wife, happy life.' These days, this seems quite old fashioned, somewhat insulting and full of cognitive bias. The kernel of truth behind it, however, relates to something Zig Ziglar said. 'You can get everything in life you want if you will just help enough other people get what they want.'

To achieve this, though, you have to move from a focus on *me* to a focus on *we*. My friend Janine Garner wrote a book, called *From Me to We*, on this very concept. You might also call it switching from 'attention in' to 'attention out.' It's what great leaders do; they move from *being great* to helping *others to become great*.

We are firmly entrenched in a period of egotistical narcissism. Much of it based on little more than 'this is how I feel today.' Lots of opinions, lots of sharing, lots of 'look at me.' There is plenty of freedom to self-express, but not a lot of encouragement to self-regulate.

You don't disappear in service to others; rather you turn up in service to others.

I used to worry that this culture of self-absorption was dooming our society. Yet, I have come to realise that it is part of the classic cycle of maturity. We grow from the belief that 'it's all about me;' to wanting others to 'look at me;' to

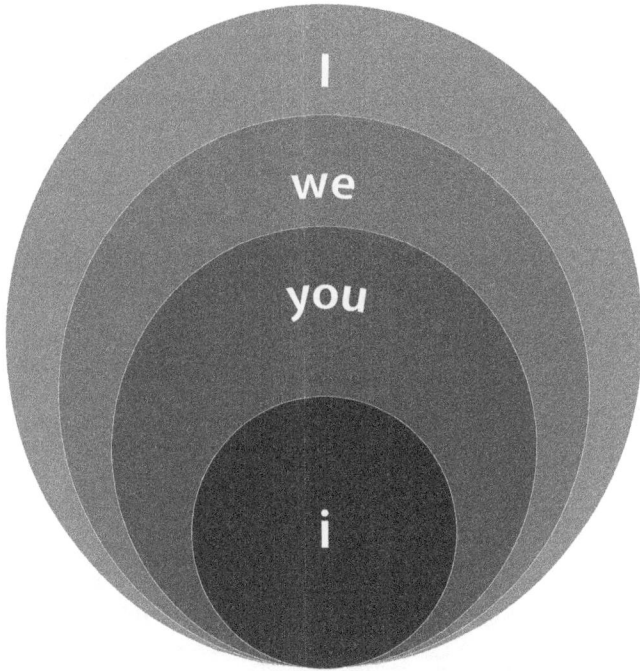

Figure 7. **Little i to Big I**

finding that 'you and me' is what is essential; then 'it's all about you;' and ultimately, 'there is no me' where we live within an entirely new consciousness.

Although you might be led to think otherwise, you don't *disappear* in service to others; you *turn up in* service to others. In my book, *Amplifiers*, I used the terms 'i,' 'you,' 'we' and big 'I' to discuss where our focus is on the path to becoming a leader who works in service of others.

For most, the little 'i' inherent in a new or solo business, becomes an accusing 'you' as we instruct others. From this point, nothing happens until we, as leaders, start to shift the team into a powerful 'we' and we all work together. And when we do this work in service to others? We end up in big 'I,' and that's where the magic happens.

Here are some stepping stones that will help you elevate yourself:

If you are caught up in little 'i' know this:

- It's OK to be scared; just don't let fear run your life.

- You are correct. We can all see that you are scared and no amount of blaming, shaming or complaining will hide it from an evolved other.

- Because we know you are scared, we stand back and let you run around breaking and hurting everyone around you.

- We indulge your personal stories and your bias because we have to, not because we want to.

- Your drama doesn't matter, and so we let you have your tantrums.

- We can see how exhausted you are and even though we want to help you, you make it so difficult for us to do.

- Chill out. It's not always about you.

- Put down your paranoia, drop your weapons.

- Breathe, and say these three words often: Sorry. Thank you.

If you are caught up in 'you,' know this:

- You are not always right.

- Defending your point of view is unnecessary.

- Being right is not as important as being kind.

- No one appointed you Chief Opinion Maker.

- Don't preach; teach. And only if you have experienced it first. Understand that we each need to live through our own lessons.

- Pointing fingers at others only highlights what you are deeply afraid of.

- We don't know all your secrets, and they don't matter to us.

- Stop competing with everyone; it's not always a race.

- What you do to one of us, you also do to yourself and all of us.

- Go deep inside yourself and heal the hurting little kid. Tell your seven-year-old self that it's OK. You were doing the best you could with what you had at the time, and it's not your fault.

- And again, for those in the back, *it is not your fault.*

- Practice letting go and surrendering. Try going with the flow for a bit.

- Work on being patient and slowing down.

So, now that's done, can we start to work together, please?

While the first two stages are about *opinions* and *thoughts*, the next two are about *space*. Get into the space of *we*, not *me*, and from there, you will begin to experience the power of being big '*I*.'

Great leaders switch from being great to helping others to become great.

The most significant realisation occurs when you realise that you are part of something bigger than you. An egocentric view of the world is statistically flawed. How could one person in 7.4 billion matter as much as you sometimes think you do? It makes no sense. Part of this 'something bigger' is how we experience our self in relationship to others. We need to realise that the learnings of this life are often found in the desired and denied elements of our relationships. It is in service to others, that we will thrive.

These four simple ideas might make the path easier:

Say thank you

Focus on gratitude as a tool, not just a behaviour. Gratitude helps you switch attention from 'woe is me' to 'wow, thank you.' Trust me, this is a much better place to live. Russell Brand made a short video in which he talks about the selfishness of caring.

Develop empathy

In her book, *UnSelfie: Why Empathetic Kids Succeed in Our All-About-Me World*, Dr. Michele Borba, makes a case for empathy as the ultimate competitive advantage. She unpacks techniques that parents can use to help kids to become more caring and why this will matter more in a tech-centric future. This book also helps your kids to stay kind in their generation's *Lord of The Flies* culture of queen bees and wannabees.

Be about Joy

To borrow a phrase from Oprah Winfrey ask yourself, what sparked joy for you today? Find small moments of joy and be a well of freshness to others. This reflects the importance of experiencing the small things, nature, laughter and perspective. Don't take everything so seriously. In the now moment, there are no worries. It's only by projecting upon the past, and prematurely inviting the future, that we fail to be here now.

Gratitude helps you switch attention from 'woe is me' to 'wow, thank you'.

Focus on your best you

Self-reflection is an important tool for lifting yourself. Most people check their actions, in hindsight, and rate them as above or below the line of intent. If you choose to, you can rewrite your story. What happened to you is not always an indicator of what you're capable of in the future. As Jim Rohn, Tony Robbins' mentor used to state, 'your biography is not your destiny.'

It has long been my opinion that you lead best when the best version of *you* talks to the best version of *us*. To be your best self, work towards the big 'I.'

ONLINE REFERENCES

Brand, R., *Selfish Pigs In A Selfish World!* https://www.youtube.com/watch?v=eYVY9S52ZkA

BOOKS MENTIONED

Borba, M., 2017. *UnSelfie: Why Empathetic Kids Succeed in Our All-About-Me World*. United States: Simon & Schuster.

Church, M., 2013. *Amplifiers: The Power of Motivational Leadership to Inspire and Influence*. Australia: John Wiley and Sons Australia.

Garner, J., 2015. *From Me to We: Why commercial collaboration is the key to future proofing business, leadership and personal success*. Australia: Wiley.

QUESTIONS

1 Where does insecurity turn up in your world?

_____

_____

_____

2 Is there a domain where you tend to be preachy and talking at others?

_____

_____

_____

3 What can you do in approach and style to be more inclusive of others?

_____

_____

_____

4 Can you recall a time when you felt it was safe to be you without conditions?

_____

_____

_____

5 Describe the experience, what did you do, how did you feel, what were the preconditions that made that possible?

_____

_____

_____

THE EVOLVED MIND

Toxic tribalism and identity politics are responses to the fear that people feel in this decade of disruption and century of transformation. The generalised fear and anxiety is causing people to cluster around 'like' and this, as history has shown, is a recipe for disaster. For a society to evolve, for the culture you lead to future-proof itself, you must drive a diversity and inclusiveness agenda. Not everybody agrees philosophically with me on this and that's OK. From what I can tell, groupthink, could be the single greatest threat threat to the way in which a collective, in all its forms, thrives.

Many different philosophies and methodologies are used to categorise and label people. From star signs to Myers Briggs profiles, these are attempts at creating models of the world and therefore have both strengths and flaws. This idea was well illustrated by the statistician George Box, who famously said, 'all models are wrong, but some are useful.'

The ideas addressed in this chapter are no exception, and similarly, it too will have its flaws. But the intent is good – to embrace difference! The diversity model here should help you let go of some unhelpful world views and level up as a leadership group.

The trick is to use world views as frameworks, rather than truths. If it is useful, use it. Just don't let it use you. This appropriate disrespect demands that you 'Hold on tight with an open palm' as the Zen koan says.

The evolved mind paradox

The idea that your world view could be flexible is possibly one of the hardest things to grasp. In my mind, it is the primary anchor that keeps us attached to who we have been and prevents us from going to the next level as leaders. Dr Bob Bays teaches in his *Identity Factor* course, that the moment we realise we can choose our beliefs, is the moment we begin to live a more successful life.

But what if you are leading people with dramatically different world views to yours? It's most definitely going to happen, needs to happen and is what leadership demands happen. When it occurs, it's worth taking a moment and realising that a belief is simply a thought you continue to have. The sign of an evolved mind is the ability to handle contradiction, ambiguity and paradox. To entertain two opposing ideas at the same time is uncomfortable, discombobulating and counter-instinctive. Yet it is the key to growth and leadership.

When your world-view defines your self-view, the idea of entertaining a different point of view puts your very identity at risk. However, what you think of as your identity – the thing that you think is you – is not. Our identification with caste, race, age, gender, national-ity, birth order, star sign, theology or profession is socially wired into us. In our mind at least, that is who we are. So the idea of entertaining difference and embracing diversity is biologically counterintuitive.

Working to elevate the D&I agenda in and around your life, business and team is a crucial adaptation skill in the 21st century.

Put simply, Diversity and Inclusion (D&I) increases compet-itive advantage. Groupthink, fixed mindsets and generational beliefs limit all you can be and all you can do. Consciously questioning and then working to elevate the D&I agenda in and around your life, business and team is a crucial adaptation skill in the 21st cen-tury. There are a series of steps that must be taken to implement this model (see Figure 8).

We evolved to defend our way of life and to 'tribe' (as a verb), sharing a collective world view as a way of surviving and then thriv-ing as communities. Like attracts like. But aren't we now beyond the survivalist ideas that birthed nationalism and fuelled world wars? Trump, Xi Jinping and Putin still leave us to wonder.

Historian David Christian, in his Big History Project, places the history of humanity in the broader context of the universe's history. The Big History Project calls this idea of establishing world views as 'Threshold 6; Collective learning.' Spend some time on the Big History Project site with kids; it is great stuff.

Adopting world views

It is efficient to adopt a certain belief to help make up your mind. Just as long as you don't believe that any particular view holds for everyone. There will always be at least one other person on the planet who thinks something different. The world is flat because we are

5	**Worldviews**	*A state of non-judgement and pure acceptance of other's beliefs.*
4	**Mind**	*The end game needs to be exploring different worldviews, different inner dialogues.*
3	**Age**	*Both ends of the time continuum serve. Old and fresh experiences create a rich combinatory play.*
2	**Gender**	*Both nature nurture create differences between men and women. Leverage the differences.*
1	**Ethnicity**	*Culture is powerful when we learn from it rather than dominate it.*

Figure 8. **D&I Levels of Evolution**

the centre of the universe – until we realise, 'Oh OK, it is actually a sphere that is circling the sun.'

Humans are extraordinary meaning-making machines. It was part of our evolution and survival as a species to make sense of something by wrapping a narrative or world view around it. This ability enabled us to leapfrog over generations of biological evolution and to adapt to a changing world. First within centuries, then within generations and soon, possibly, within decades. The thing is, though, our meanings are not the truth. They are simply useful.

> *The sign of an evolved mind is the ability to handle contradiction, ambiguity and paradox.*

Dogma is powerful because it creates a control dynamic that eliminates the need for self-reflection and self-regulation; systems take the guesswork out of living. The choices are made for you, and this makes life easy. Follow the rules, work within the system, and you will be fine.

The problem is, many of us are over being controlled or told what to do. Our systems and institutions have failed us. They have lost our trust, and yet most of them would say to us that we have just lost our faith. It's a clever and convenient meme; all you need to do is plant a seed of doubt and fear causes most to fall back into the fold. To be controlled.

When world views collide

Freedom is the one goal we are all searching for, yet it comes with enormous responsibility. Intolerance, such as that demonstrated by ISIS or the KKK, comes from clashes in ideology and world view. The fight to impose a world view on others and to control some part of the species through labels is historically evident. Nazis and Jews. Apartheid in South Africa. The Crusades. And on it goes, with one world view claiming supremacy over another. It's horrifying when viewed historically. Create a world view, teach it to others, defend it aggressively, and you get to control the masses.

And yet despite philosophical, theological and psychological inferences, it is not about the rightness or wrongness of any one world view over another. The idea of D&I is about you taking things up a notch. Of being the best version of yourself, as defined by yourself. So be fluid with world views, selecting and discarding them as they lose their usefulness. For me, it comes down to a simple question; does operating within this framework liberate or restrict me? As long as it works for you, keep working it. When you start having to work for it, maybe it's time to let it go.

Fixed world views lack behavioural flexibility. That rigidity allows good people to let bad things happen, or for evil deeds to be swept under the table. At the very least, it reduces commercial agility. Fixed world views are not nimble enough to disrupt themselves, change their approach midstream and give up on ideas, products or services that are no longer relevant. Unfix your models of the world, as they and you are unbelievable.

Kimberle Crenshaw's Ted Talk on intersectionality explains to me the importance of mindset as the meta dynamic at play around a legitimate D&I strategy and the evolving of mind. Another approach is the short talk by Tibetan monk Dzongsar Khyentse Rinpoche about Homosexuality and Buddhism. As a middle aged, middle class, white male, I don't pretend to any experience or expertise in these areas and remain a student on the journey of awareness in all things.

ONLINE REFERENCES

Bays. B., http://www.drbobbays.com/shop/the-identity-factor

Big History Project. https://www.bighistoryproject.com

Box, G. E. P. (1976),'Science and statistics' (PDF), *Journal of the American Statistical Association*, 71: 791–799, doi:10.1080/01621459.1976.10480949.

Crenshaw, K., https://www.ted.com/talks/kimberle_crenshaw_the_urgency_of_intersectionality

Rinpoche, DK., https://www.youtube.com/watch?v=qA_Kp9v9ZtA

QUESTIONS

1   Can you name one paradox that you think about often or that drives your life?

_____

_____

_____

2   Can you recall a belief you once held to be true that is no longer so?

_____

_____

_____

3   If you have a precious belief, explore a set of circumstances where that may no longer apply?

_____

_____

_____

4   Where does having a strong belief in something serve you?

_____

_____

_____

5   And where does having a strong belief in something not serve you?

_____

_____

_____

THE DEADLOCK OF DOGMA

In the last chapter, the diversity and inclusiveness agenda was elevated. The top of the model presented mindset and world views. This is where true diversity lies; not in your age, gender or ethnicity but rather in how you think and see the world. Dogma and doctrine are the tools of division, and evolved leaders, creating world-class businesses and lives, will develop an allergic reaction to the 'should' and 'must' of dogma. Evolved leaders have risen to the challenge of curiosity and openness. They break the deadlock of dogma and doctrine.

everal years ago, I was identified as being an introvert on one of those personality type tests. Have you ever been identified as X or Y and then found yourself living according to that label? Living into the identity stories created for us by others?

Chloe, my 18-year-old daughter, delivered her last speech as School Captain. She has proved herself to be an extraordinary leader and there was a message in her address that I love.

> 'We spend so much time trying to find ourselves at school. Am I popular? Am I smart? Am I arty, dancy, sporty? The truth is that you are none of these things. You are something deeper, truer and less impermanent than *the labels of identity* we adopt and carry throughout our school career. Allow your light to shine (school motto) by focusing on what is true, not just what is new. I reckon the greatest gift we can give another is the gift of seeing them for who they are, not just what society expects them to be.'

This notion of *the labels of identity* resonated deeply. I told Chloe I want to be on her staff when she runs Greenpeace 2.0 or the Intergalactic United Nations. *Ad Astra*, Chloe.

Wearing binary coloured goggles gives you a very limited view of life.

British singer, Sam Smith, recently came out as identifying as non-binary. Their music makes a powerful declaration to rise above labels. I started to watch Dr Jordan Peterson's response to the legalislated use of non-binary pronouns in Canada. There is heated opinion surrounding the issue of gender identification. I published some thoughts around this to a list of leaders who read what I write and received some very interesting responses.

But what's all this heat about? It's clearly not about gender.

I think fear and control are driving any anti-PC backlash in this issue. A meme that is currently travelling the internet role plays a fictitious conversation between someone and the personification of political correctness. It's helpful here.

Someone: 'I hate political correctness!'

Political correctness: 'I prefer to be called 'compassion''

Someone: 'Yeah, but that makes it harder for me to say I hate it!'

Compassion: 'I understand.'

Discussing this with my friend, Michael, who is also the designer of this book, his response was not to ask yourself is something PC, but rather is it kind?

It seems that many people feel safe and 'in control' with absolutes. Black, White. Friend, Foe. Love, Hate. Good, Evil. Male, Female. I don't believe life is that binary, that clear-cut, that convenient. Wearing binary coloured goggles gives you a very limited view of life.

Whenever given a binary choice or an ultimatum, I find myself assertively seeking to confuse the dogmatic perspective. The more adamant the viewpoint, the less I buy into it. This rejection of absolutes seems to be cross-generational and is on the rise in today's youth. Power on.

Go ahead, be yourself.
Be whoever you want.

It's pretty simple. What do you want and need from me? If there is no obligation or compromise, then 'Whatevs', 'Be who you want to be, do what you want to do, yeah.' Let's stop telling each other who to be or what to do and let's just meet each other wherever we are at. Maybe life will offer more wonder and delight as a result?

Diversity and inclusiveness are bigger than ethnicity, gender or age. It's about the wondrous variety that is present in our world. After all, variety is the spice of life. Life would taste pretty bland without it.

Go ahead, be yourself. Be whoever you want or need to be.

The Habit of Three

As a leader, there is a way to break the deadlock caused by dogma.

You can develop the habit of three.

Comedians know that three average jokes create a bigger laugh than one cracker joke. Dr King, Obama and JFK built their speeches around three core ideas and three comments related to each point. A three-by-three matrix is the perfect strategic map, and it creates the ideal formula for message management.

My friend, Col, thinks that when it comes to meetings, three is the right number of attendees. Amazon founder, Jeff Bezos believes that if two pizzas can't feed the attendees, you have too many people in the meeting. Three people, three slices each (and a few to go in the fridge for lunch the next day). Three topics discussed, three decisions made. In my mind, this is the perfect symmetry of three.

Develop the habit of three.

Three is good.

1. Three kills duality.

Two is not a choice; it's an ultimatum. Ultimatums are fundamentally binary, e.g. on/off, yes/no, hot/cold. I'm glad that when I was a kid, they didn't have most of the labels and diagnoses that kids get pasted with today. If they'd had words for it back then, I would have been diagnosed as having Oppositional Defiant Disorder. If you tell me 'no', I find myself drawn to ignore that directive just to be noncompliant. I suspect that few of us like to have our options reduced to two uncreative and inadequate binary choices. Three breaks duality in the simplest way.

2. Three creates movement.

The role of a leader can be defined as reducing fear and replacing it with confidence, removing confusion and replacing it with certainty and mobilising people in pursuit of a better future. Three elements, three ideas, three messages, three stages. Three provides mental momentum. Unpacking three concepts in a sequence overcomes resistance and inertia and creates a compulsion to act.

3. Three builds diversity.

Two might be an accident. If we give two ideas, two demographics, two stereotypes, our audience thinks 'coincidence.' Three is design. The deliberate use of a third person, example, type or idea communicates range and breadth (or at least the start of it). Three proves your point.

Some historically famous threesomes:

Father – Son – Holy Ghost

Bronze – Silver – Gold

Body – Mind – Soul

Head – Heart – Hands

Race to the future – War for talent – Battle for Attention

Matter – Meaning – Meta

It's as easy as A – B – C…

Three is good.

Develop the habit of three.

ONLINE REFERENCES

Smith, S. https://www.bbc.com/news/newsbeat-47612616

Peterson, J. https://www.bbc.com/news/world-us-canada-37875695

BOOKS MENTIONED

Hawkins, D.R., 2005. *Truth vs. Falsehood: How to Tell the Difference.* 1st ed. United States: Veritas Publishing.

QUESTIONS

1 Can you recall a time when you had a major
difference of opinion with someone?

_____

_____

_____

2 Was there a set of operating rules they were breaking?

_____

_____

_____

3 How does having a set way of operating serve you?

_____

_____

_____

4 How does having a set way of operating hinder you?

_____

_____

_____

5 Where in your life or business does dogma exist?

_____

_____

_____

THE TRUTH AS WE KNOW IT

Deeply philosophical and yet highly practical is the discussion around levels of truth in this chapter. This chapter calls leaders to act with integrity, and not apply the asymmetry of knowledge in their quest to be the best or get to the top. Manipulating the truth is how many have achieved and maintained power, and it's a seductive cup. This chapter explores the application of truth versus falsehood and gives some pointers to how you can hold the higher ground.

Who knows anything, right? Seriously, almost anything a person says is true, is true for them but may not be absolutely true. What do we really know to be true? It's such an interesting question and one that has started philosophical debates and ended many a friendship. The truth is both absolute and relative, and there are fewer of the former and maybe too many of the latter.

Stay with me; this chapter is going to get a bit out there. You may want to skip this chapter as I suspect it's where we split into two groups. Those who think, hell I am out of here and those who go, hold on, this shit is starting to get real. It's OK whatever choice you make, but this chapter is a bit of a line in the sand.

Let's see if I can ground it to start.

In behavioural science, the Observer Effect is the awareness that people change their behaviour when they know they are being observed. If you asked whether they were being dishonest or misrepresenting the truth, they would swear they are not. Interestingly in quantum science, the Observer Effect is a described as a known phenomenon, wherein an electron will behave like a wave if you look at it through a wave detector and as a particle if you view it through a particle detector. That's right: it is correct to call an electron both a wave and a particle. So what really is an electron?

Newtonian physics has a different set of operating rules to Einsteinian special relativity, which is different again to those of quantum mechanics. I don't pretend to understand the differences. But those I trust to know explain that the truths are different in each field, and each is accurate within its context. Be careful what you say is true – perhaps it is true for now or true in this situation, but is it indeed true?

As you journey up and out, as you Rise, you begin to see that the pursuit of the truth is a powerful thing; perhaps the only thing you need. In business and in relationships many hide the truth through lies of omission or hide the truth in the name of commerce, or negotiation.

The Truth	Something that is true in all situations and for all beings	Absolute truth
Personal	Something that is true for you but may not be true for another	Relative truth
Dodgy	A truth that is strictly true but intentionally deceptive	Whipped cream
Polite	The truth we withhold so as not to hurt another	Little lies
Repressed	The passive-aggressive truths we share	Bitter truths
Omission	The lies we tell contained within partial truths	Lies of omission
Self Deceit	The lies we tell ourselves that we hold to be true	Self delusions
Deceit	The lies we tell ourselves or others that we know to be lies	Outright lies

Figure 9. **Levels of truth**

Mother Theresa asked the wealthy of India for money but chose not to tell them it was for the untouchables. She felt the ends justified the means. That starts a whole ethics debate that I am not that interested in or qualified to discuss. While there is less that's absolutely true than we think, there are many things that are relatively true.

Be gentle with what you think is true; hold lightly to it.

Leaders are often expected to be keepers of the truth. I think it might be better to be seekers. On a very pragmatic level, this is commercially smart, as Twain (supposedly) said 'It's not what you don't know that will kill you, it's what you know to be true that just isn't so.' Be gentle with what you think is true; hold lightly to it. What is true below the line is no longer true above the line.

Focusing on the truth becomes a game wherein you allow for the shifting of world views, flexibility around core values and beliefs, and the willingness to not know much at all. Not knowing, not having an opinion, is how you open up to what might actually be true. The opposite of this unknowing state is the battle to push some dogma on others. That includes pretty much all theisms. Apart from the manipulative, controlling nature of dogma and doctrine, the arrogance of its absoluteness stops progress. It puts a ceiling on the Rise of a group of people.

Dr Hawkins writes in *Truth Versus Falsehood*, that the minute the truth is institutionalised, it starts to become something less than it was. He references this in the context of many religious doctrines. Similarly, history shows that the lifecycle of many businesses is to go from a fluid, agile start-up, able to respond to new ideas only to then morph into a supposedly safe, structurally locked up entity. These fixed, rigid entities, ironically prevent the creativity of the very people that made it something worth embracing. There are exceptions to this doomed fixed narrative and yet there are enough examples of it being true as to lend some commercial wisdom to the idea that putting something into a cage of efficiency may be the worst thing to do.

Truth is a similar idea. Stay open to what you perceive as true; it may be that you are looking at the electron through the wrong instrument. When we cage and institutionalise the truth, we make it into a specific something, perhaps a rule, a belief or an opinion. We change its form from a truth to a falsehood.

SBNR

When my daughter Chloe started high school, I was delighted to see an application form option against the question of Religion that I did not recognise. The menu options were things like: Option 1 – Anglican; Option 2 – Presbyterian; Option 8 – Atheist. But it was option seven that got me interested.

Religion: Option 7 – SBNR

I had no idea what option seven meant, so I asked the school administrator. It turns out that SBNR stands for *Spiritual But Not Religious*. It's a legitimate choice for those who feel there is something other than us, an infinite intelligence of sorts, but don't identify with any particular religion. Turns out that's me. This book has elements of many different spiritual traditions; I am interested in any place or writing that feels like truth to me, and yet do not feel the need to join their club. Groucho Marx said it so well when he said, 'I would never be a member of a club that would have me.'

For over 25 years, I would have identified as an atheist. Then one day, I woke up to a recognition that that belief no longer held for me. It's amazing how much energy gets caught in the body of identity, both within me and with others. This realisation has caused some concern with people near and dear, as who they thought I was, their label of my truth, was no longer stable.

The best way I can describe it is that I gave up the fight to believe that I did not believe. I finally surrendered to the truth that all my life, I have been guided by a gentle love within me for everyone and everything. This realisation woke in me a desire to return to love.

Many of my SBNR friends, when asked if they believe in God, will say 'Yes, God is in me as me.' When pushed for what they believe in, most will answer 'the truth' and when asked how to prove that God exists will say 'you can't.' You can't prove God exists, so in a way, everyone is, at best, agnostic. But you can know the experience of God as a quiet, loving presence behind your thoughts. Those are the words many SBNRs will use.

So as a leader, the truth as you know it may not be the truth. The truth that someone is prepared to die for may not be the truth. Depending on how you view a subject, the truth might change.

My truth is that I am not the voice in my head, and neither are you. You are the truth that sits behind the awareness of that voice. It's a bit Zen and perhaps not appreciated in a leadership book. But I don't reckon I want to hold it back anymore. If you are going to listen to anything, then I say you might as well know what sits behind the saying.

BOOKS MENTIONED

Hawkins, D.R., 2005. *Truth vs. Falsehood: How to Tell the Difference.* 1st ed. United States: Veritas Publishing.

Williamson, M., *Return To Love.* United States: HarperCollins.

QUESTIONS

1 Talk through the eight levels of truth with someone and discuss how they feel about being the receiver of a certain level?

_____

_____

_____

2 Do you find yourself at any of these levels of truth more than another?

_____

_____

_____

3 What do you know for sure to be true? (and how do you know that?)

_____

_____

_____

4 What do you know for sure is not true? (and how do you know that?)

_____

_____

_____

5 Google quotes on truth. What's your favourite? Discuss these with key people you live or work with.

_____

_____

_____

THE LAST LECTURE

This final chapter in Part One asks you to delve into the DNA that will inform your personal leadership vision. We know leaders share visions that compel us towards exciting and new futures. What is yours based on? This chapter unpacks what your epic origin story could be. You need to win the race to the future, the war for talent and the battle for attention. You need to move from simply informing us of your plan and your vision, to inspiring us towards it. Act as if it all matters, this chapter explores how to do that.

Many universities ask their professors to give hypothetical 'last lectures', summing up the lessons that they have learnt over a lifetime of teaching and learning. Dr. Randy Pausch, a computer science university professor, knew he was dying of an incurable illness and had only months to live. His last lecture was not so hypothetical.

Upon learning of his illness, Randy decided that he would not go quietly into the night. Instead, he committed to making his last days on earth extraordinary. He would be present, connected and loving. Instead of talking about dying, he talked about living.

His presentation, and subsequent book, entitled *The Last Lecture* are indescribably elegant.

It's worth asking yourself a similar question and taking time to explore what matters most to you. If you had one lecture left in your life to give, what would the message be? How would you sum up the lessons that you have learnt over your lifetime?

We are often asked to write a reverse eulogy; this is your own story told at an imagined funeral service in your honour. A mentor recently challenged me to write my memoir in two sentences. This reminds me of Spike Milligan's request that his tombstone read: 'I told you I was dead.' Mel Brooks wrote 'that's all folks,' and Sinatra wanted 'the best is yet to come.' But it's Sir Winston Churchill's that I like most. 'I am ready to meet my Maker. Whether my Maker is prepared for the great ordeal of meeting me is another matter.'

We are all more than we allow ourselves to believe.

Maybe mine might say, 'I'll see you everywhere, in all things, at all times.'

So what would yours say?

Then take a moment and write your memoir. Here is an example.

My Memoir

The story I am about to tell is based heavily in the world of make-believe. It's a story of the journey through greatness, not towards it. It is the realisation that everything we experience in this expanding universe we call life, is mirrored by a deep connection to something other, or more accurately, something more than this. We are all more than we allow ourselves to believe, and yet ironically we are often desperate to be seen as a certain something, shifting and shaping our narrative to project a skin to the world that suits.[1]

All great stories are based in conflict and remembered in truths. The conflict in this story is between fear and love, reality and deep reality, and loving, leading and living above or below the line. This is truly a story of make-believe as we as humans turn on our universal superpower to create and make meaning everywhere we go.[2]

Jim Carrey explained it well in a commencement address at Maharishi University of Management, when he said, 'You can fail doing what you don't want, so you might as well have a go at doing what you do want.'[3] The truths that drive this story are ancient and as such, should be mistrusted. Memes and ideologies are fundamentally flawed and therefore are useful until they're not.[4] Many lay criticism at the feet of flawed perspectives, rather than enjoying the work it took to create that view, enjoying without binging.

If a story lay on a spectrum where on one side we have educated opinion and the other enlightened insight, then the dance between these two is a tension between logos and ethos.[5] The hero of this story is a slave to the third lens, pathos. The balance between the internalised emotion of self-interest answering the question 'Does this feel good?' and the arrogance of compassion in 'First do no harm' and ultimately an obsession to 'develop greatness' both within and without. Attention out, loving, leading, parenting and mentoring others so that the best version of you talks to the best version of us. A lifetime pursuit worth chasing, and the driver behind this hero's call to adventure.[6]

This story is one of convenient beliefs, helpful delusions and borrowed worldviews. Indeed, a slippery, appropriate disrespect for dogma is the golden thread that runs through every chapter of this story. To some extent, the story is redundant if the following universal truths are understood, and as such I will write this introduction only and leave the story alone. Discarding the husk of the hero's journey for you to fill in your own as you create your life.

For in the end there is a wonderful lightening of the burden of living when you realise that you are no-thing. Not from a nihilistic perspective of insignificance that abandons all hope agnostically, but rather one more like the Buddhist idea of interbeing.[7] If I am in you and you are in me, then the pinched off self we call 'me' is less narcissistically relevant.[8] Rumi, the 13th-century Persian poet, captured it beautifully when he said 'you are not a drop in the ocean but rather the whole ocean in a drop.'

So a story full of contrast, but remembered in the following temporary truths.

The Temporary Truths

1. It's all make believe. What do you choose to believe in this moment? Is that belief helping or hindering you? If a belief is merely a thought we continue to have, are yours serving you?

2. You are the creator of all that you experience. Don't give up your power and become a slave to the drama triangle of human experience.[9] You are not broken, you are not better or worse than any other. You don't need saving, and you need not rescue others. Make yourself (and others) strong, not wrong.

3. State matters more than script so determine who you are being in each moment by choosing your response to any given set of circumstances. Indeed, it never matters what

happens to you, it's how you respond to it that matters. In this way you maintain your agency, your locus of control.[10]

4. Love is the killer app[11] and as such know that the stronger you get, the more gentle you become. Buddha said that 'Love is the recognition of yourself in others and delight in the discovery,'[12] so look for more moments when you can declare that you are the other, not separated from the other.

5. You are the creator. You are the god, the life force that has sat above and within numerous religious societies. The day you realise this and behave *as* God is the day you graduate from the life–death cycle that runs most people's patterns.

So...

Up and Out.

Get 'above the line' and 'be attention out'.

There is greatness in you.

Namaste.

ATTRIBUTION MARKS

Ideas are meant to be shared and often they are borrowed in such a way that direct in copy/conversation attribution is clumsy. In the above text such attributions are indexed in this list. I am calling these attribution marks as a way of demonstrating the importance of signalling where your ideas are born. Not in an egoic preservation of source but rather so that those who wish can go deeper than my collapsed summary on an idea that catches their mind.

1. Peter Gabrielle introduces a song *More Than This* and the soundtrack is a great musical accompaniment to this post. https://www.youtube.com/watch?v=IK0HmAvoUgQ

2. I am often inspired by the work of my friend Michael Henderson and suggest his book *Above The Line* and the work of the late Dr Hawkins, specifically the work of *Power vs. Force*.
Henderson, M., 2014. *Above the Line: How to Create a Company Culture that Engages Employees, Delights Customers and Delivers Results.* Australia: John Wiley Sons Australia Ltd.
Hawkins, D.R., 2014. *Power vs. Force: The Hidden Determinants of Human Behaviour.* United States: Hay House Inc.

3. I suspect that comedian Jim Carrey is popping consciously and moving from satire to spirituality. Interestingly, critics suggest that he is going mad, a remark that is neither useful nor original. Conspiracy theorists would suggest that historically wisdom that breaks the bubble, reveals the matrix is labelled as a kind of madness. Maybe that's the ultimate red pill (The Matrix) moment. https://www.youtube.com/watch?v=V80-gPkpH6M

4. Memes. An idea postulated by evolutionary biologist Richard Dawkins.
Dawkins, R., 2006. *The God Delusion.* Australia: Transworld Publishers Ltd.

5. Logos, Pathos and Ethos. Aristotle's artistic proofs.
http://pathosethoslogos.com/

6. Joseph Campbell's hero's journey is unpacked in his book, *The Hero With a Thousand Faces*, and is stimulating defined as the monomyth. http://mythologyteacher.com/documents/TheHeroJourney.pdf

7. The Buddhist idea of interbeing is explored here in an interview with Zen monk, Thích Nhất Hạnh. https://tricycle.org/magazine/interbeing-thich-nhat-hanh-interview/

8. 'Pinched off' is a wonderful phrase used by spirituality teacher and 'collective consciousness channeler' Esther Hicks.

9. Drama Triangle is a life-changing idea explored by many. This is the reference to the only book on the drama triangle written by the original creator Dr Stephen Karpman.
    Karpman, S., 2014. *A Game Free Life - The definitive book on the Drama Triangle and Compassion Triangle by the originator and author.* United States: Drama Triangle Publications.

10. This is a reference to the key idea in *Mans Search for Meaning*.
    Frankl, Viktor E. 1984. *Man's search for meaning: an introduction to logotherapy.* New York: Simon & Schuster.

11. Tim Sanders said this and titled a book of the same name. https://www.fastcompany.com/44541/love-killer-app

12. My favourite Thích Nhất Hạnh quote.

ONLINE REFERENCES

Pausch, R. talk: https://www.youtube.com/watch?v=ji5_MqicxSo&vl=en

BOOKS MENTIONED

Pausch, R., & Zaslow, J. 2008. *The Last Lecture: lessons in living.* United Kingdom: Hodder & Stoughton.

QUESTIONS

1 Google good tombstone quotes, what's your favourite?

_____

_____

_____

2 How would your one-line eulogy read?

_____

_____

_____

3 Where do you believe you have agency
and control in your life?

_____

_____

_____

4 Where do you think agency and control
are lacking in your life?

_____

_____

_____

5 If you had one last lecture to give, what
would be your three lessons on life?

_____

_____

_____

PART TWO

A NEW CONTEXT

Folk law has it that a professor at a business school once asked the students to imagine that they own a store that sells drills. With this artifice established, she then asked them to name in as few words as possible what business they were in. Some said advice, some said construction. The professor heard them out and then revealed that perhaps they were in the business of making holes. She went on to suggest that if someone came up with a better way to do that, they had better stop selling drills. Context provides a freedom that content does not, at a business and a personal level. Shift your business context and perhaps the ultimate context, awareness.

Shift your context professionally

As the world shifts from bits to bytes, from products to services, from owned to shared, we need to rethink our business models. Re-examine the way we operate contextually. Imagine that the primary way you make money got taken away, disrupted or deregulated in some way. What would you do next? How can you thrive through disruption?

Sometimes it's not even the doom and gloom of disruption that drives the shift; it's an opportunistic piece of positioning. What business are you really in? Can you pivot or adjust your model towards a different focus? Transforming business, industries and yourself as a leader, means being willing to shift from one context to another.

I'll start easy in this chapter by keeping it focused on the objective nature of business. Then I will turn the same idea onto your personal operating context. Buckle up – this one might get bumpy.

Jamie Pride is the author of *Unicorn Tears* and a great thought leader around startups, entrepreneurial spirit, and how founders thrive (or not). He once explained to me Kimberly-Clark's pivot from standard nappies into pull-ups as a shift from a business built on 'dryness', to one focused on 'shame'. Rather than an either/or, they developed an and/also business. The big word that drove their business was adapted to include another big word. They added a new context to their existing one.

A big part of leading is listening, connecting and being present. The monkey mind can prevent that.

In his book *Free; the future of a radical price*, Chris Anderson, the founding editor of *Wired* magazine, explores the seismic shifts in ownership and pricing. He unpacks an example of jazz musicians in Brazil, who found their concerts recorded by music pirates and then sold on the footpath as their audiences came out from the show. Instead of fighting the thievery, they sent high-quality 'glass masters' to the bootleggers so that they could duplicate brilliant recordings. The musicians then enlisted the bootleggers to sell tickets to their shows. When your business of selling CDs becomes putting on shows, the problem becomes a solution. Once again, they changed their context or word, thereby improving their business.

A key part of becoming attention-out is stilling the non-stop soundtrack.

Many celebrities indeed make as much money appearing at clubs and events, as they do selling their craft. Indeed, since Paris Hilton, the Typhoid Mary of reality shows, 'appearance money' has driven a whole new entertainment genre in reality TV. Miss Hilton was one of the first to be famous for being famous.

I used to think I was in the *idea* business, but I realise now that I am in the business of *experiences*. In the idea business, you defend your intellectual property, package up your ideas into books, CDs and membership sites, and become an expert in SEO, copyrighting and stranger marketing. I decided that like the bands in Brazil or Paris Hilton (don't judge me), you can take a Matt Church idea and claim it's yours, but it's very hard for you to be Matt Church and to replicate a Matt Church experience. This pivot towards a different or new context is how you adapt and thrive in a disrupted world.

At a recent conference, one of the speakers shared how the top ten companies in the FT500 in 1997 were vastly different to those in 2017 (see page 100). He referenced this Economist article which claims that data is the new oil. These days, more IP businesses are built around services and fewer around being asset-rich. Their big word has moved from *asset* to *data*.

We see this in the shift online from *search* to *social*. A change in words, a variation in context is one of the most powerful ways to change the game, disrupt your market or make an impact. Your big word becomes a lens through which you see the world, make a

2007		2017
General Electric	1	Apple
Royal Dutch Shell	2	Alphabet (Google)
Microsoft	3	Microsoft
Exxon Mobil	4	Amazon
Coca Cola	5	Berkshire Hathaway
Intel	6	Exxon Mobil
Nippon T & T	7	Johnson & Johnson
Merck	8	Facebook
Toyota	9	JP Morgan Chase
Novartis	10	Wells Fargo

Source: Financial Times 500

Figure 10. **World's biggest companies 2007 & 2017**

difference and make mistakes. When you question that contextual lens, you can begin to evolve and drive change.

Maybe you need to change your business context. Perhaps you can extend it or add to it. One thing I know for sure is that leadership teams need to be having these conversations *before* they start to explore strategy. The business context changes your primary questions, eliminates the need to be everything for everybody, and gives you a lens through which to see the world and make decisions.

Shift your context personally

So the question is, 'Can you see the Matrix, Neo?' Are you currently operating in a limited framework as a person or as a leader? Here is another deep, personal example of how context shapes everything.

Do you talk to yourself? If not, who just asked that question?

We all have a voice in our head, an incessant voice that drives what is often called our stream of consciousness. Meditation and many spiritual practices have particular activities, like chanting 'Nam Myo Renge Kho', that aim to still the busy, always-on mind. In Buddhism, this state of mind is affectionately referred to as the monkey mind. If you have ever spent time near a troop of monkeys, you understand how relentlessly chatty they can be. It is distracting and hard to focus on anything else in their presence.

A big part of leading is listening, connecting and being present. The monkey mind can prevent that. Rehearsing what you are going to say then constantly reliving what you have said, can prevent you from being present and concentrating on what is unfolding right in front of you, right now. As you've probably guessed, the monkey mind contrasts with the calm, centred, still and blissfully quiet mind of a Monk.

Here are the two states of mind compared side by side:

Monkey	Monk
Noisy	Quiet
Anxious	Calm
Controlling	Allowing
Paranoid	Certain
Busy	Relaxed
DO-ing	BE-coming
(past) **Driven** (future)	(now) **Present** (now)

Figure 11. **Monkey or the Monk**

Sigmund Freud famously defined the Id, the Ego and the Super Ego. This triadic distinction was expanded on by Carl Jung and others. We could also talk about the anima, the shadow and other theories. If you are into such ideas, then I imagine you have already been there and read that. Either way, consider this. There is the 'you having a thought' and there is the 'you observing you having a thought'. This idea has been labelled metacognition and is something Aristotle wrote about.

I am in you,
and you are in me.
Thus any attempt to
control, change or
influence another
is a form of madness.

In education fields, this is well-researched and often labelled higher-order thinking skills. It drives a fabulous focus on getting beyond rote learning and creating a transfer in learning. For over 50 years, Project Zero, out of Harvard University, has been working on classroom curriculums and developing thinking dispositions. They make all kinds of suggestions, such as monitoring the learning, not the work. Concentrating on what you think the teacher wants you to learn here (learning) versus what the teacher asks you to get done (work). They are getting us to think about thinking, and to develop habits of the mind.

A key part of becoming attention-out is stilling the non-stop soundtrack. It's the stream of consciousness that gets in the way of the wind in the trees, the soul in the back seat, and even the human by your side. Get above the noise and quiet the monkey mind. As Jung wrote, 'Until you make the unconscious conscious, it will direct your life, and you will call it fate.' Learn how to catch yourself out when you are building scripts that only revisit the past or rehearse the future, and spend more time staying in the now. Two excellent books on being present include *The Power of Now*, by Eckhart Tolle and *Be Here Now*, by Harvard professor turned Guru, Ram Dass.

Staying in the now helps to still the monkey mind. That voice in your head has no shame and will happily take you anywhere. Focus on almost anything, and and it may speak in a way that is violent and unhelpful. While many awareness disciplines teach you to fight the ego, making an enemy of your thinking is not helpful, even if the attacking nature of some thoughts is counterproductive to your leadership experience.

Attack thoughts

One way the monkey mind takes over is when we start to have negative attacking thoughts about others. For this to happen, you need to create a separation between me and you, us and them. Any time we see ourselves as separate; we enact a form of violence. It's not the same as physically hitting someone, but it can have similar energy for anyone sensitive to the declaration of Self as other. At a relative level of truth, you are you, and I am me. At a level of absolute truth, at least for some, you are in me, and I am in you. We live better when we are in love with the divine essence that exists in each of us. The 'I' in 'I am' is your divine nature. The Hindu greeting 'Namaste' literally means, 'I see the God in you.'

When I say something about you, it's an opinion; when I share something about me, it's my relative truth. Neither case is likely to be the real truth. We often define ourselves in opposition to others. Judgement, comparison, feedback, opinions and preferences are all forms of attack. I am me, you are you, and you or I are not good enough. Accepting the perfection of what is, means you agree that everything is as it should be. It is as it is. Admitting the is-ness of any moment, means stepping out of the world of duality, and into the nonlinear world of deep loving presence. This is what it means to Rise Up and lead.

At the heart of this is the idea that there is one behind the two. I am in you, and you are in me. Thus any attempt to control, change or influence another is a form of madness. Why would I control me?

To what end? It's insane, a grand delusion. By shifting the context of your awareness from separate to same, from you and me to us, you get to experience new things in your life. If you are not the voice in your head, then what are you? This question sits at the heart of the Zen enquiry into consciousness. Shift your context, and you change your world. And this is where the idea gets very, very, commercial.

Think about changing your perspective, adding a new one or completely changing the direction of your primary operating setting. Your business tells a story that sits within a broader environment. So too, the stories you tell yourself fit within a particular framework. A whole new mind arises when you look through a new lens. You are not the voice in your head, and of course, the Monkey mind is not a truth. It's just another story.

ONLINE REFERENCES

Project Zero. http://www.pz.harvard.edu/projects/visible-thinking

Economist. https://www.economist.com/leaders/2017/05/06/the-worlds-most-valuable-resource-is-no-longer-oil-but-data

BOOKS MENTIONED

Anderson, C., 2009. *Free: The Future of a Radical Price.* United States: Hyperion New York.

Dass, R., 1974. *Be Here Now.* United States: Harmony.

Pride, J., 2018. *Unicorn Tears – Why Startups Fail and How To Avoid It.* Australia: John Wiley & Sons.

Tolle, E., 1997. *The Power of Now: A Guide to Spiritual Enlightenment.* Canada: Namaste Publishing.

QUESTIONS

1 What business are you in?

_____
_____
_____

2 If a disrupter entered your sector, how would they answer the same question?

_____
_____
_____

3 What business could you be in?
(name three alternatives)

_____
_____
_____

4 How aware are you of your internal dialogue?

_____
_____
_____

5 What's the tone of that dialogue?
(Does it serve or sabotage you)

_____
_____
_____

THINK YOURSELF FREE

If you are not your thoughts, then how do you liberate yourself from the continuous internal dialogue identified in the last chapter as the Monkey mind? You could use deep insight as a means of personal liberation. The tyranny of the undisciplined mind is propped up with half-baked ideas; semi considered concepts and incomplete thoughts. The monkey mind has little shame or discipline. Pink sheeting your thoughts helps you place them outside of you. We use that for commercial gain as thought leaders; equally you can use the practice to liberate your Self from the thoughts in your head

Were you ever taught to think?

Imagine you are invited into a quiet room and given the instruction to do some thinking. What would you do?

Would you pull out a pen and notepad?

Would you sketch out a mind map on a tablet?

Would you sit still and concentrate on your breathing?

Would you look for some stimulation by searching the web?

And at the end of that time what would you have to show for your deliberate thinking? Could we take that thinking, put a price on it and share it with others?

It's all a bit hit or miss, isn't it?

If we asked you to reflect on your schooling; when were you taught to think? We really weren't. So here it is. The Pink Sheet Process is a way of thinking deeply and deliberately about something. We are sure it's not the only way to think and maybe not the best way – although we suspect that perhaps it is. Without a doubt, it's a very effective way to think; to capture and flesh out your ideas.

Thinking consciously

For many of us, when we think we find ourselves reflecting on a past event or planning for a future one. The question is: 'Are you consciously thinking?' or is the monkey mind running things? The monkey mind being that noisy, reactive, paranoid, jibber jabber that passes for a stream of consciousness.

Often, when teaching the idea of pink sheets, we are struck by how hard it is to get your head around a straightforward idea, how to sit down and think deliberately about something.

We realised that teaching this is a bit like teaching meditation or mindfulness. It's through the practice of meditation that you get better at it. Similarly, it's through the practice and application of this thinking process that you get better at thinking.

One of my virtual mentors is Thích Nhất Hạnh. He teaches mindfulness so that you learn how to fill your mind with the present

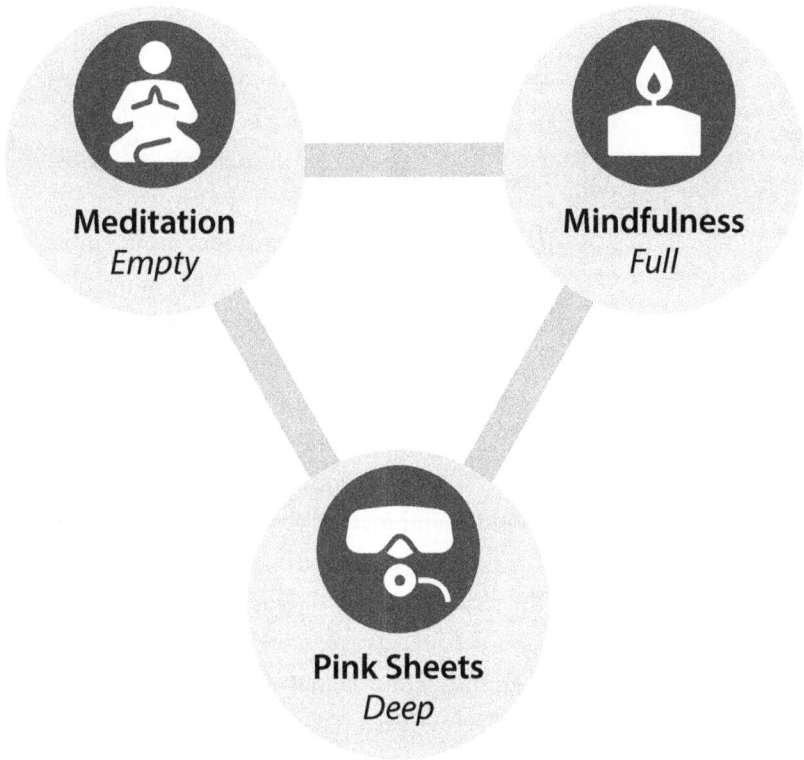

Figure 12. **Meditation, Mindfulness and Pink Sheets**

moment. It is about eating, walking, breathing, sitting, listening and being fully present to what's in front of you.

It may be useful to consider meditation and mindfulness on a spectrum. On one side, meditation is about emptying your mind, releasing thoughts and focusing on very little. On the other side, mindfulness is about filling your mind and the act of deep sensory immersion. It's probably truer, though, that meditation and mindfulness become the same thing over time: a state of being present. If we then took this idea further, the process of pink sheeting is the third element of a triangle. It becomes about opening your mind, contemplating an idea and focusing on solving a problem – something Buddhism calls deep insight.

Using the Pink Sheet framework to capture your ideas creates depth in your thinking. It forces you to create messages with substance and balance.

It could look like the model on page 111. This is a simple idea that is often hard to grasp. It's not that it's complicated – it's just not our usual state. As in meditation and mindfulness training, however, it is something you can get better at through regular practice.

An introduction to Pink Sheets

So what is this thing we are calling a pink sheet? A pink sheet is a tool we have been teaching thought leaders for decades (see page 113).

Why is it called a pink sheet? One of the first times I taught this tool, there happened to be pink paper in the printer. In that workshop, they got dubbed pink sheets, and the name stuck.

Perhaps we should have come up with something bit more profound? Another more highbrow way of defining a pink sheet is to call it an intellectual property snapshot. Since then people have come up with a dozen reasons why it's on a pink sheet. Pink equals think, a

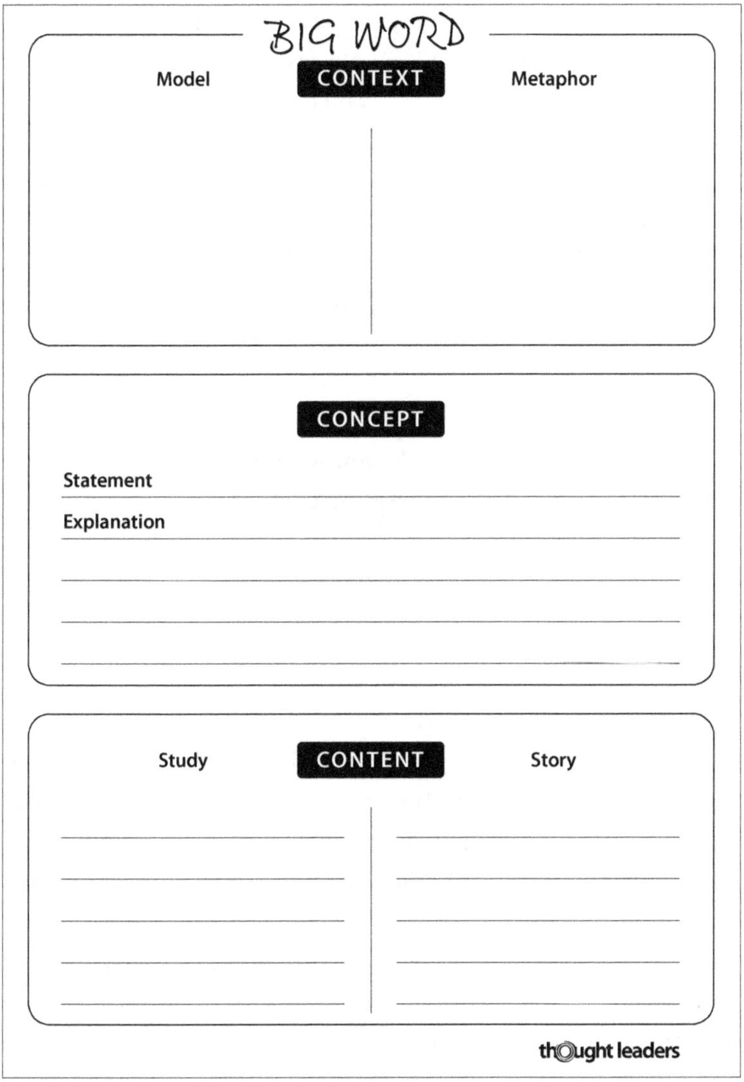

Figure 13. **Pink Sheet**

pink slip is a certification of property registration, and this is intellectual property. A pink slip is an old-fashioned payslip and, if you want to get paid for your ideas, you need to get pink sheets. But really it was a printing error that stuck. And like all nicknames, once you are labelled, it's hard to change. So, pink it is!

The Pink Sheet Process is a way of thinking deeply and deliberately about something.

Using the Pink Sheet framework to capture your ideas creates depth in your thinking. It forces you to create messages with substance and balance. Each concept or point you want to share will have its own pink sheet.

Concept

Start in the middle of the page.

Your concept lives in the middle of the Pink Sheet and summarises the point of the idea. The goal of this section is to make you select your words carefully. As thought leaders, we need to make statements memorable, to craft great ideas into powerful memes that spread. The concept layer of the pink sheet is where this process happens. There are three primary ideation strategies we recommend to make this work. You can do one, two, or all three of them. Each will stretch your mind in different directions, with the goal being to uncover something special that you didn't realise you had in you.

Firstly, start a journal and witness what happens to you during the day. Ask yourself as you do this, 'What have I discovered or learnt today?' The second strategy involves reading research papers and books on a topic of interest and when you go to highlight something ask yourself 'What do I think about this?' The third idea is to search for quotes on your area of interest and play with extending or contradicting the premise behind the quote. Ask yourself 'Yes and if we took that further then…' or 'No, that doesn't apply in this scenario because…'

Context

At the top of the pink sheet is context, the overarching theme within which this idea lives. Context is characterised by three parts:

The model

The model is a diagram which describes where this idea lives in the greater hierarchy. It might be a Venn diagram, or a ladder, or a circle. It's a tool which visually describes the hierarchy of ideas in play and provides a map for navigating them. A single model will often be the parent of (and therefore shared across) a number of pink sheets. A five-rung ladder model would lead to at least five pink sheets.

The metaphor

Metaphors are an incredibly powerful way to help people relate to an idea and immediately understand its relationship to the wider issue in play. They allow the brain to use existing neural pathways and cognitive understanding and apply it in the new context. As a tool for gaining rapid understanding of the significance and importance of an idea, the metaphor is invaluable. Some metaphors will be shared across multiple pink sheets. Some will apply only to one. In his book, *I've Never Metaphor I Didn't Like*, Mardy Grothe unpacks the history of the most enduring metaphors and offers hundreds of examples from famous thinkers and writers that might stimulate your own ideas.

The big word

This is the overarching theme of the idea. If you could use only a single word to describe the significance of the idea, then that is the word you would place here. It's the word that will help you group appropriate pink sheets together when you're crafting your speech.

Content

The bottom layer of the pink sheet contains the stuff. Here's where the supporting data, case studies, stories, anecdotes and pictures live. Remember that each point should be represented as much as possible by left-brain analytical content such as data and case studies, along with right-brain creative content, like stories and anecdotes. Ensuring you have a variety of content across the spectrum means you'll be well equipped to back up each point with compelling and relevant content, cherry-picked to suit the audience.

One of the key takeaways for you to consider when learning this IP snapshot process is understanding the layers of thought. There are small ideas—detail and content—which rise through layers of abstraction to the higher levels of understanding. For example:

Small: Hamburger

Medium: Food

Big: Energy

The hamburger is the concrete detail of the idea, but the higher context to consider when hamburgers are in the conversation is energy. Learning to identify the higher contextual ideas that frame your content, and successfully communicate it with your audience, will massively increase the strength of your presentations. It helps dispel disagreements of the 'he said, she said' kind that tend to be mired in detail and achieve little or nothing. It links each of your points into a bigger, more convincing overall argument that more people can understand and identify with. It groups your points into congruent families that share common themes and build off each other.

So, for each of your ideas, you'll need to work out where on the pink sheet, the idea lives. Is what you've got the equivalent of 'hamburger', 'food', or 'energy'? Is it content, concept, or context? 'red bus', 'transport' or 'movement'? Do you need to think up or down (or both) from this starting point? Have you recorded a basic story

	COMPONENT	EXAMPLE	APPLICATION
1 **CONTEXT**	**Left brain context**	Model	*Gain consensus*
2 **CONTEXT**	**Right brain context**	Metaphor	*Embed understanding*
3 **CONCEPT**	**Key point or meaning**	Concept	*Cut to the chase*
4 **CONTENT**	**Logical evidence**	Case study	*Back it up*
5 **CONTENT**	**Emotional engagement**	Story	*Make it memorable*

Figure 14. **The five components of an idea
and their application**

(right brain, content)? Have you drawn a model (left brain, context)? Thought of a metaphor (right brain, context)?

Once you've figured this out, you'll know what thinking still needs to be done. You may find that some of your ideas belong together on one pink sheet. Perhaps a workplace story beautifully illustrates a concept statement from elsewhere. Maybe several separate points can be tied together into a single overarching model.

It's good to be light in this process. Don't be too concerned with detail and locking things down. Aspire to be playful and try lots of different ways of arranging and connecting information. You may be surprised by what wisdom hides within your mind, waiting to be unlocked by the process of stretching yourself out of your usual mode of thinking (see page 117).

Practice is the key. As soon as you can wrap your head around it, have a go at a pink sheet. I suggest you use the process on someone else's ideas first. Learn the process of capturing a concept you already know but did not come up, with on a pink sheet.

Learn more at the Pink Sheet Process website!

Concept Reveal

I was asked at dinner, what would I say to the Thought Leaders tribe if I had to do a mic drop moment; a last message to them all. I instantly knew the core idea I would share, and it's revealed in the opening frame of this chapter; Using deliberate thinking to end thinking.

If you spend enough time pulling ideas out of your head and seeing them as constructed opinions, you get to the point where you start to dream in pink sheets, think, listen and read in the language of a pink sheet. Then you become free of the tyranny of your own opinions. You see ideas and opinions for the constructs that they are. This gives you a certain detached lightness with them, and if you immerse yourself in the process over time, you see the process as a gateway away from the noisy, insistent thinking that leads to suffering. I used pink sheets as therapy for a busy mind and found that on the other side of deliberate, commercial, strategic thinking was a profound peace of mind.

ONLINE REFERENCES

Pink Sheet Process. https://www.pinksheetprocess.com

BOOKS MENTIONED

Grothe, M., 2008. *I Never Metaphor I Didn't Like: A Comprehensive Compilation of History's Greatest Analogies, Metaphors, and Similes.* United States: Harper Collins Publishers.

QUESTIONS

1 What do you know about meditation?

_____

_____

_____

2 Have you ever practiced mindfulness?

_____

_____

_____

3 What does deliberate thinking look like to you?

_____

_____

_____

4 Can you explain someone else's big idea using the pink sheet? (give it a go)

_____

_____

_____

5 Can you name the five elements of a pink sheet and identify your personal preferences?

_____

_____

_____

MULTIPLY YOUR INFLUENCE

At some point, you may choose to get very, very good at addressing large groups of people. It is both a science and an art and one worthy of study. It is also a way to calibrate where you are at on your journey up and out. You can think a thought easily enough; it's when you express it out loud with many witnesses that the stakes go up. We need more evolved leaders on the public stage. I have thought for some time that when evolved leaders talk into a community; the vibration of that community lifts. Like the effect of a rising tide on all ships in the harbour, your transmission as a leader has a positive impact on others.

T here will come a moment as a Risen leader where you will realise the need to speak out en masse. A time when you choose to take your *personal influence* skills, and turn them into *multiplier* skills. One obvious way to do this is to become a better public speaker. My book *Speakership* is a great resource to get you focused on the fact that *who you are being* as a public speaker matters as much, if not more, than *what you are saying*.

All my books, including *Speakership*, are digitally free to download from my website. This chapter should act as a short activator to the idea that speaking matters.

The case for public speaking

We live in a hyper-connected world, more plugged in, tuned in, turned on than ever before. Everything we need to know is just a swipe away on a mobile device the size of your hand that has more computer power than NASA when it put two men on the moon in 1969. Want to know the temperature in Brazil right now? The price of wool in Otago? How about finding an old friend from high school? Most likely, they are just a google search away. The world has most certainly shrunk.

And yet, social scientists tell us that more and more people feel isolated and disconnected from their communities. They feel overworked, underpaid, misunderstood and alone. Despite the capability to be in touch twenty four hours a day, seven days a week, many people are disengaged and disillusioned. Business leaders know the struggle to engage and empower a workforce that, in large chunks, clock in and then checks out.

The new leadership imperative is speakership.

Speakership is leading out loud. It's the leadership equivalent of management by wandering around. Visible leaders, influencing and inspiring their people to action by sharing messages that matter. Speakership is the partnership of powerful memes and masterful oration. James Hume, the presidential speechwriter for Ronald

Reagan, once said, 'Speakership is leadership, and every time you are speaking in public you are auditioning for a leadership position.'

For all the incredible discoveries that the written word has enabled, it has limitations. Firstly, as a source of inspiration and influence, it appeals only to a portion of a population. Right before a big game, world-class coaches don't send a well-crafted memo to their players. They get into the changing room and deliver powerhouse speeches.

Speakership is leading out loud.

As incredible as an idea can be, the written word is rarely as compelling as when delivered personally, with conviction. If you want to tell someone you love them, you look directly into their eyes and say those three magic words. Out loud.

For business leaders, creating clarity from confusion, turning fear into confidence and mobilising your people to act in pursuit of your shared goals and direction is at the very heart of what you do. You can't lead your team into battle with an underwhelming whisper.

Those who can articulate the way forward, who inspire with powerful messages, who motivate and provide clarity and make meaning when they speak; these will be the leaders of the near future. Your ability to step up and cut through the noise of mass media, to provoke new insights, to challenge the status quo and bring every group you speak to closer to the central vision of your organisation is what will set you apart.

You've got to get good, really good, at speakership; sharing your voice to larger and larger groups.

You've got to get really good at spreading messages that matter; sharing your ideas with the world.

The idea that you influence those around you by the quality of your ideas, and the conviction with which you deliver them is not new. History is steeped in the rallying cries of great men and women who have stood up and led, out loud. In doing so, they brought others together to build movements and campaigns that have, quite literally changed the world.

As we write this, the most popular TED talk of all time, Sir Ken Robinson's treatise on schools killing creativity in children, has been viewed 62 million times, and not always just by a single person at their computer. It's been shown in groups, classrooms, conferences and more. Consider the impact that 20-minute presentation has had around the globe. Think of the number of lives that will be different (and better) as a result of that meme being powerfully shared with educators the world over. This is a shining example of speakership. If the only thing Sir Ken did in his life was to deliver that speech, he would have had more impact on the world than 99% of all people that have ever lived.

Now more than ever, we need inspired leaders who inspire us, challenging leaders who challenge us. Now more than ever, speakership is leadership.

In business and life, mastery of speakership creates opportunity and impact. Those willing to invest the time and effort into developing their speakership skills will inevitability find themselves with more opportunities, more invitations and the growing confidence to take those opportunities in both hands. There isn't a personal development programme in the world that will accelerate your leadership growth more than committing to standing on a stage, or at the front of the meeting room, and auditioning to lead.

As you journey further along the path you will start to get more and more comfortable speaking in public, as your identity becomes less and less important. I like the metaphor that your egoic self dissolves. Great speakers focus their attention on different things.

When we start out speaking in public we can be a little self-conscious, and the little voice of criticism seems to find a new audience and stage. You may have silenced, or at least quietened that voice in your day to day interactions with others, but the multiplication of

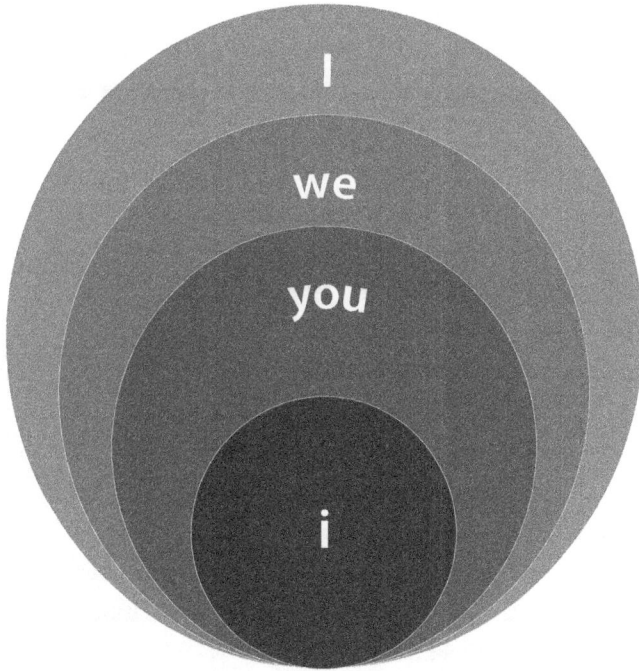

Figure 15. **Little i to Big I**

message, amplification of self and witness of others creates a potent new platform to explore your focus and attention.

Speaking in public creates a new place for you to test your detachment and concern for the good opinion of others. The collective scrutiny can drop you a level or so. This is natural and one of the reasons you would choose to run into the burning building that your fear conjures up at the thought of speaking in public. It is akin to the belief that while it might be easier to practice Zen in a temple, it may be useful to practice it on a busy street. The little *i* in this model, speaks to the moment when your internal dialogue is plagued by monkey mind thoughts, expectations and beliefs. You are not these thoughts. Rise Up.

In an attempt to connect with others, it's possible to become separate and create walls between yourself and your audience. A preachy, teachy style, delivers sermons from the mount. Standing behind a lectern, holding on for grim life, finger-pointing, looking down on the audience. Your job is not to do anything to us as an audience. You do you, we will do us, and where the two intersect in service to a greater good, true connection will occur. If you find yourself standing apart and aside from your audience, remember this; act as if the audience is you. Remove the walls of separation and fix any nervous tension with a service orientation. Don't get lost in the *you* orientation.

The collective *we* is where you begin to deliver the Leadership implied in the word Speakership. Use inclusive language, involve the audience and work to make people feel part of the conversation as opposed to receiving a presentation. Put your Powerpoint to one side. If you do use slides, make them visual and a backdrop to your communication, as opposed to a script you read out in front of a crowd. Get out from behind your slides and create a conversation, not a presentation.

The next layer of attention in the Speakership model is to focus on the *message*. Message describes the information you're sharing with the world. Not just the value of the message, but the elegance with which it is constructed and described. The greatest idea on earth has no value if no-one understands or remembers it. A truly powerful message is carefully designed to be easily digested and understood by people with a full spectrum of life experiences, motivations, and learning styles. A truly powerful message is one that is illustrated beautifully with models and metaphors, woven into compelling stories, and supported by empirical

Now more than ever we need inspired leaders who inspire us.

evidence. A truly powerful message can be learned quickly by the audience and shared, creating a meme with lasting impact.

At some point, you will start to feel like your messages are coming through you and not actually from you. This seems to occur as a subtle emergence in most people. It's not a dramatic explosion where one minute you have agency over ideas, and the next they possess you.

The way you deliver your message is the *method*. This encompasses your skill in delivering your content with flair and purpose. It means you use humour, movement, stories, characters and drama to deliver your message in a manner that increases audience engagement and information retention. Method means having all the tools and techniques to capture and maintain the attention of an audience and deliver the message in an entertaining and memorable fashion. Beyond simple party tricks, or the indefinable personality trait *charisma*, mastering method means knowing when and how to use any and all of these tools and techniques to deliver the message with maximum impact.

The *Big I* is the awareness that occurs at a level of *mastery*. Once you have the capacity to know yourself, the audience and the space that exists between you, you can start to work on powerful messages that are well delivered. All of these stages create, over time, a condition wherein you can speak to a group of people and have a kind of out of body experience. You feel like you are watching yourself delivering a presentation. This shift in awareness and non-personal identification is the start of the journey into the Big I, what many call the self with a capital S.

It's a little like the intuition that is born from experience. Think of the way a world-class tennis player can read subtle cues from their opposition and make adjustments to their swing without even being conscious of noticing the cue in the first place. That's not possible when you're a beginner, and your mind is flooded with thoughts of grip, swing, foot movement, shot selection and strategy. Like winning Wimbledon, the journey to speakership mastery is not one that will happen overnight.

It's a path that takes time to tread, and experiences along the way play an important role in your development. There will be successes, and inevitably failures; the only certainty is that at some point you will need to speak before you are ready. Comedian Steven Wright once said, 'Experience is something you don't get until just after you need it,' and it's hard to imagine a domain outside of public speaking where that statement rings truer. Mastery is only possible when you are so in control of your message and method that you create space in your consciousness for even greater awareness of what's happening around you.

So where to start?

It doesn't so much matter what you say, as who you are when you say it. As you rise up and begin to explore truth as you know it, you will speak from a state of awareness that goes beyond the simple rational thought of a prepared speech. You will still prepare, but you will do so to be in a flowing conversation with your audience. You lead best when the best version of you speaks to the best version of us.

The rest is admin.

ONLINE REFERENCES

TED. 2006. Ken Robinson: Do schools kill creativity? https://www.ted.com/talks/ken_robinson_says_schools_kill_creativity

BOOKS MENTIONED

Church, M., Coburn, S., & Fink, C., 2017. *Speakership*. Australia: Thought Leaders Publishing.

QUESTIONS

1 **How do you feel about speaking in public?**

_____
_____
_____

2 **Where on the little i to big I journey are you, when you speak in public?**

_____
_____
_____

3 **What's your favourite Ted talk and why?**

_____
_____
_____

4 **What do you enjoy about a speech when you are in the audience?**

_____
_____
_____

5 **What do you not enjoy in a speech when you are in the audience?**

_____
_____
_____

NOT WORTHY

At some point along this journey, perhaps even now, you may have a crisis of confidence. A moment of doubt, when the edges of your identity and capability meet. We start to look out at others, with one eye turned inwards and finding us lacking. The paradigm that prevails follows a lot of the historically negative, self-help, personal development banter. It says that you are somehow broken and in need of fixing. That sells courses but does very little for your ability to evolve and grow as a leader and a person.

My opening comments to this book were essentially about a crisis of confidence. I had serious doubts about whether I could, should or would be able to write this book. While it's not gone as far as it might, the messages have gone beyond where I have historically felt comfortable. It's a stretch for me and thus a moment to answer the call to Rise Up. I predict this might happen to you, too, at certain points on your journey.

There are at least three different angles for addressing the 'Not good enough' story. One is to contribute rather than compare. One is to surrender to the humility of your limitations. And the last is to use the power of forgiveness to access the non-judgmental space of acceptance.

Contribution versus Comparison

When you have a not good enough story going on in your head, it may be based on comparison to others or expectation of yourself. This is such a game of make-believe. You often find out that you are ten times better than you believe yourself to be, and that whoever you are elevating on a pedestal has psychological demons and challenges of their own. It's often remarked that if everyone were to put their life dramas in a pile on display in the middle of a room, we would all say 'Ah, shit, no thanks, I'll keep mine.' The grass on the other side of the fence is probably gravel.

At Thought Leaders, we encourage every person to write a book during their first 18 months of a three-year programme. Most often, a student will go into a bookstore, search all the books on their chosen subject and instantly be overwhelmed by the number and calibre of volumes already published. This is hugely demotivating, as you begin to ask, '*Who am I to write on this? It's already been done, and so much of it is awesome. If anyone had time to read on the subject, they should read Book X or Book Y before they even get to my book.*'

And this is true and valid.

We spend so much time trying to be great—*'My book is a best seller'*—or unique—*'No one has written on this!'*—that we forget our job is to be of service. Somewhere, six people might get something from your book, and it might help them on their journey, so get on with it. Your job is not to decide if you are unique or popular, your job is to do the best you can with what you have, for whomever it helps. Contribution serves us better than comparison.

Acknowledge the assist

Sometimes you need to surrender to the humility of your limitations. This is such a powerful quality that it's easy to think of it as not bragging about your accomplishments. While on one level that's true, it also means you put down the expectation that you deserve the glory for any achievement.

In the US National Basketball League, there is an idea that many coaches think defines a team's culture. It embodies the spirit of surrendering to your limitations. In the 1960s a conversation between Coach Dean Smith and Coach John Wooden started what has now evolved into a powerful tradition amongst basketball superstars. Two world-class coaches, Smith and Wooden, wanted to

Contribution serves us better than comparison.

initiate an explicit gesture that would make personal success overtly linked to team efforts. It became pretty simple; when they scored, players were asked to acknowledge whoever passed them the ball, by pointing a finger at them. If you scored then point to the passer and in doing so, you acknowledge the assist. Smith made this a formal part of the North Carolina men's basketball team culture. As time went on, he rolled it out beyond baskets to misses and screens. The bottom line was that he wanted his stars to share the glory, regardless of the outcome.

Many superstar players thank the pass or acknowledge the assist and also point to the sky, recognising that they alone are not in charge. In Latin, the phrase *In Excelsis Deo*, Glory Be to God, speaks to this. It's not about your stance on Jesus, Gautama, Mohammad or Moses; it's about moving the glory and praise away from your personality and identity.

The ancient Romans believed that you had a team of incorporeal geniuses who served you in this life. I find it helpful to think that greatness comes through me, not from me. Yes, that's a particular world view, but it serves me not only as an orientation to life, but also to do and be more. This approach allows me to get over myself and do stuff that matters, that makes a difference, that scares me or for which I feel unworthy. It works for me to surrender to something bigger.

In Thought Leaders, we help a lot of clever people to be commercially smart, and as such, there is a lot of talent flying around. Plenty of superstars. Chiefing a tribe like this takes finesse. One quality that has worked is aligned with surrendering to the humility of your limitations. Akin to acknowledging the assist, this means committing to the habit of attribution and developing a disposition to elevate others.

A community devoted to developing great ideas could become a place where it's unsafe to share your thoughts. Someone might take your brilliance and pass it off as theirs. Indeed two members of our community were recently in a legal stoush around who owned a certain word. It made me very, very, sad. No one owns ideas, so set them free. They were never yours, anyway. Plagiarism is fear-based and most definitely a 'below the line' concern. We work hard to ensure that thought leaders acknowledge the giants on whose shoulders their thinking developed. Rigorous, disciplined, institutionalised, attribution and acknowledgment are critical when talented, smart people are collaborating. Watch the humility as the rising tide lifts all ships, as hubris will sink a few.

As a leader, your job is to help others rise. The disposition towards elevating others is a learned habit. We love praise so much as little children that we can become greedy for it. Within you and your team, the inclination to elevate others and point out what makes them extraordinary is a good one. Surround yourself with greatness and get out of the way.

If you wish to be a leader, if you wish to Rise Up, you will need to let go.

A great leader is one who can bring greatness out in others. For this to happen, the best version of you needs to speak to the best version of us. On my YouTube channel, you can find a lecture from 1972 delivered by Holocaust survivor Victor Frankl, the author of Man's Search for Meaning. This short video, delivered to a youth group in Canada, is witty and charming. In it he quotes Johann Wolfgang von Goethe, 'If we take man as he is, we make him worse. But if we take him as he should be, then we make him capable of becoming what he can be.'

My leadership lesson has been learning to manage the disappointment trap when people don't become all they could be. For what it is worth, that's our problem, not theirs? I'm hoping that it's not too paradoxical, in light of the Goethe quote, to state that everyone is perfect as they are. It's our expectations of who they should be that creates disappointment. And here is where expectations become a little ambiguous or complex. Without hope, we don't progress, and yet the very act of progress has an inherent drive to become more, to be better. Expectations and comparisons are guaranteed to make you unhappy. Learning to be light on yourself and others while wishing them to be the best version of themselves is quite mature. It's something you may wrestle with if you are on an upward trajectory. Learning the art of forgiveness might help.

The Forgiveness Project

In keeping with attribution, it's worth stating clearly that pretty much anything I present or share is derivative. I don't say that as a plagiarism disclaimer but rather as a profound truth. In my world view, ideas pass through you and don't come from you. I always feel it helps you as a reader, student, seeker or leader to know the perspective through which someone gives advice. Making my perspective explicit allows you as a reader to retain your agency. I was taught to approach any point of view with an open mind. And at the same time, never to give up my power to an idea or authority. So remember these ideas are not mine and only let in the bits that serve you. Try them on; it's your experience with ideas that matters, not my opinion.

The final approach for handling the question 'am I worthy?' is to accept that you are probably not. Know that you have done things and had things done to you from which it is hard to come back. If you want to Rise Up you need to fall onto your knees with humility and start a journey towards forgiveness.

To forgive or not, becomes the question. In his book, *Chiefing Your Tribe*, my friend and teacher, the anthropologist Michael Henderson, says that chiefs forgive with ease. If you wish to be a leader, to Rise Up, you will need to let go. Putting down stories, baggage and narratives from the past is key to what leadership expert Rohan Dredge calls a *leadershift*. Your rise into leadership is made buoyant by the dropping of grudges.

Christ is the symbol of forgiveness, his narrative is the epic quest to live and embody it. Cheek turning and all that. Pretty much every religion on the planet has some forgiveness orientation built around empathy and compassion. The perversion of certain original scriptures towards violence is a very human activity and not one worthy of attention. No one owns this idea. Check out the image on page 141, adapted from a U2 concert backdrop advancing the co-existence movement.

See? Derivative.

For me, at least, it is the Buddhists who unlock forgiveness.

Islam

No one will be a true
believer unless he
wishes for others what
he wishes for himself.

Sunnatt

Brahmanism

Never do unto others
what would hurt you
if done unto you.

Mahabharata 5 .15

Confucianism

What we do not wish
to be done to us,
let us not do it to others.

Analects 15 .23

Buddhism

Do not offend others
as you would not like
to be offended.

Udanavarga 5 .18

Judaism

What you do not wish
for yourself, do not
wish for others.

Talmud Shabbat 31 .A

Christianity

Do unto others as
you would have them
do unto you.

St. Matthew 7.12

Maya

You are myself.
We are all one.

Popol Vuh

Taoism

Make as yours the profits
of your fellow man
as well as his loss.

T'asi-shang Kin-ying P'ien

Bahai Faith

If you seek justice
choose for others what
you would choose
for yourself.

The Bayan

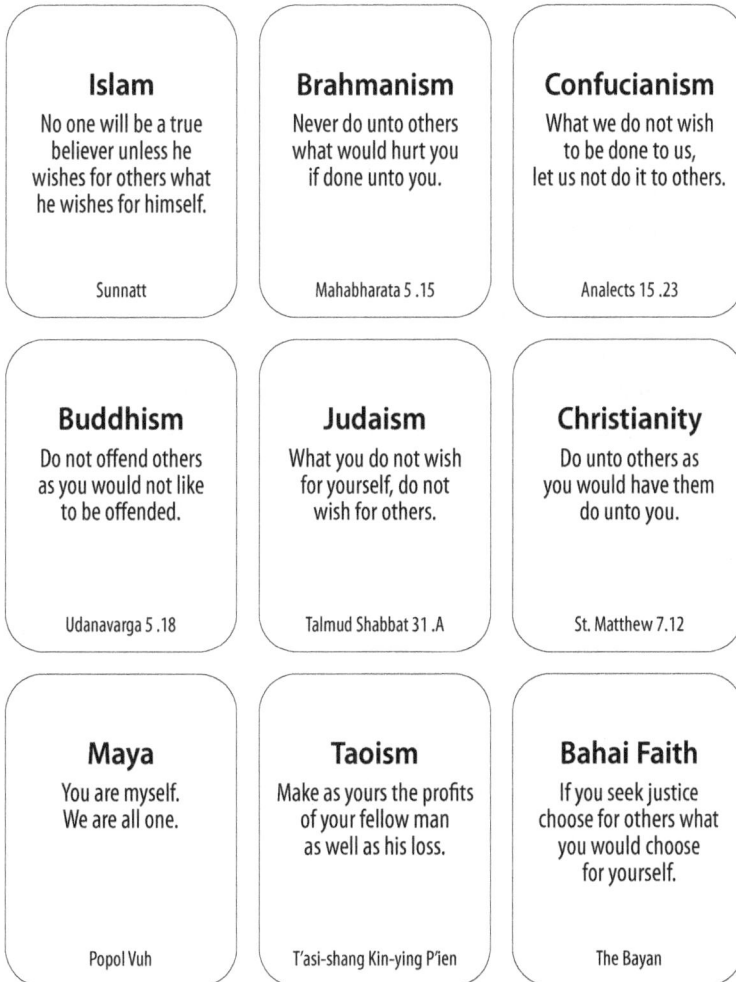

Figure 16. **Forgiveness orientation across religions**

Buddhism teaches the idea of interbeing; that I am in you and you are in me. The journey to awakening, shaped by teachers near and far, past and present, is a journey into yourself to find that you are nothing. Moving out, you realise you are everything, and finally, you become all things. As a spiritual dilettante, I find this journey; from something – to nothing – to everything – to all things, super useful. In the Buddhist worldview, there is no you and I, and as such, there is no one to blame and no one to forgive.

Buddha famously said that 'Love is the recognition of yourself in others and delight in the discovery.' And right there is the motive for forgiveness. If you accept that I am in you and vice versa, then why would I hold a grudge? A good friend wants the best for the part of you that wants the best for you. There is a self-harming quality to being without forgiveness.

Forgiveness comes about as a result of being let down by another, perhaps in a position of power. The feeling of forgiving or not is a function of an unmet need, an unfulfilled expectation. At the heart of forgiveness is the interfering quality of one over another. At the right level of consciousness, even the act of mercy is probably redundant. For me, the power of it was revolutionary. I had no idea how much hurt I have carried and caused for 50 odd years.

It was Robert, one of my teachers, who started me on the path to forgiveness. Many had told of its import, but maybe with Robert, the student was ready. He started what I have now come to term the Forgiveness Project. Robert shared that writing letters of forgiveness each night and burning them the next morning is life-changing. He was right, for 50 days and 50 nights that's what I did, sometimes writing one or two lines to everybody, or writing pages to somebody in particular. This is a good thing, and you may find it helpful. To Rise Up, you need to let go. Check out The Forgiveness Project on my YouTube Channel if you want to learn more.

Summary

You are worthy. Your job is not to be the best or better than the rest. It is to serve others to the best of your ability. Let go of the attachment that you are the one who needs to find the abilities, have the answers and always be in control. You are not. Things get better when you get out of the way. You are not qualified to judge whether you are worthy; you are unbelievable.

ONLINE REFERENCES

Church, M., https://www.youtube.com/channel/
UCY2A00uUS5yIQp6hIEXhUOA

Dredge, R., https://www.rohandredge.com

Thought Leaders Business School. https://thoughtleaders.com.au

BOOKS MENTIONED

Henderson, M., 2012. *Chiefing Your Tribe: How to Become a Leader Worth Following.* New Zealand: Author Self Published.

QUESTIONS

1 Where have you or do you have a crisis of confidence?

_____
_____
_____

2 How did you respond in that moment of truth?

_____
_____
_____

3 Is there anywhere in your life where you are allowing comparisons to stop you taking things next level?

_____
_____
_____

4 How good are you at feeding praise and credit to others?

_____
_____
_____

5 Is there anything you are holding onto that could do with a forgiveness makeover?

_____
_____
_____

BUILDING MOMENTUM

If you do have moments of doubt, if the comparisons and expectations of you become debilitating, as they have for me from time to time, it helps to have a plan of action. Keep and build the momentum towards growth and change and continuous improvement – especially when you hit a rut. It's not always a positive progression or movement up; at times, it's two steps back. This chapter looks at ways to hack the personal physics to keep moving, and perhaps in the early stages of evolution, to achieve escape velocity.

I f you want to Rise Up, you have to get up. You have to get up from the inertia of life and move. Anywhere. It's far easier to change your course when you are already moving.

The easiest way to get clear about something is to take action. Aim and fire before you're ready. While this sounds counterintuitive, it's solid advice; if in doubt, do something!

Many people spend time asking, 'What do I want?' This is a great question to ask yourself often. It's useful to recalibrate, to choose what you are creating on your life journey, and to know your motivation. But I have found that it is through an experiment or after a result, that you discover what you want. The cycle of clarity starts with action, followed by clarity and then motivation (see page 149). Not the other way around.

George Bernard Shaw said 'Life isn't about finding yourself. Life is about creating yourself.' It is through this cycle of clarity that we actively participate in the creation of our own life journey. Finding yourself is passive while creating yourself is active. Gustav Anderson, The Modern Nomad, has much to say about the wrongness of hoping to find yourself out there somewhere. Instead, we are free to evolve into something that is far more rewarding.

That's the core of success. Step up to the line, run into the fire, face down the fears and do something. But here's the thing, the rah-rah motivation of 'just do it,' doesn't cut it for most of us. Shia LaBeouf says it brilliantly in his parody of a modern performance coach or motivational speaker.

In her book *The Willpower Instinct*, Dr Kelly McGonigal does a ripping job of showing us how to get over ourselves. The team at Four-Minute Books summarise this in a one-sentence summary. 'The Willpower Instinct breaks down willpower into three categories and gives you science-backed systems to improve your self-control, break bad habits and choose long-term goals over instant gratification.' One of my favourite quotes from Dr McGonigal is that 'Chasing meaning is better for your health than trying to avoid discomfort.'

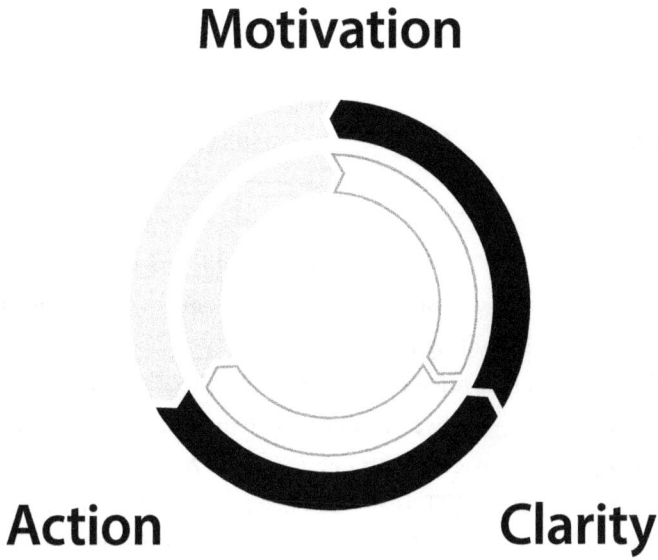

Figure 17. **Cycle of Clarity**

My friend and business partner, Peter Cook, wrote a brilliant book, *The New Rules of Management*, on how we can stack the decks in favour of getting things done. He favours building an implementation system around us. I can vouch for his premise that 90-day projects drive results. He reckons that implementing projects that matter is the only thing that matters in life. It's an excellent methodology which sits above personal

It's far easier to change your course when you are already moving.

productivity habits, explores the fragility of human will, and includes a system for really getting things done.

Dr Mike Martin once explained to me the division in performance psychology between cognitive behaviour therapy (CBT) and acceptance and commitment therapy (ACT). At the risk of over-simplification, CBT is about battling your demons through therapy and self-talk, while ACT is about finding the next actionable thing you can do and doing that. Perhaps we will see a blending of these two schools of thought in the future. At present, the CBT model is well-established in our world, while the ACT model needs greater exposure. Watch the video of Mike Martin explaining the two schools of thought and why he uses ACT with elite athletes and top performers.

It is important to remember that you don't get clear in theory, while you do get clear in practice. In his book *The Lean Startup*, Eric Ries explores the idea of a minimum viable product. In essence, an MVP is about getting something 100% out, as opposed to 100% right. Live testing, and clinical trials are part of the science of experimentation, and many breakthroughs can be found on the other side of a failed experiment.

You don't get clear by thinking and waiting for motivation. You get clear by acting. Action precedes clarity. So, don't just stand there do something.

A teenager recently asked me how to get some momentum going. As we chatted, the following model emerged, as the antidote to inertia. This advice is aimed squarely at people who are in that 'stuck' state. If you are in flow and on the move, then skip over this chapter. However, if you, or someone you know, is stuck, then these four strategies might get you moving forward (see page 152).

I shared with the teenager, that four useful habits and mindsets that distinguish those who are good at getting going. They have a sense of urgency, a growth mindset, they are good at delayed gratification, and they have nailed advanced planning. These sit on a spectrum of things you do in your mind (head) and things you do physically (hands). Some can be done immediately (now) and others have a view towards the future (then).

A sense of urgency

The first quality that inertia busters have is a sense of urgency. It's what Brian Tracy, author of *The Psychology of Achievement*, calls a bias for action. Essentially, what you are resisting is the 'I will get to that later' mindset. If you have useful workflows then delaying some stuff is smart. But if you are in a bit of a funk, then you might find having a bias for action a 'do it now' mindset – will be more helpful.

Not only do you need a sense of urgency, but you also want to do the toughest task first. Always get the biggest, ugliest thing off your plate, as soon as humanly possible. Otherwise, it lurks over everything else you are doing, and you end up easily distracted and losing focus.

Finally, develop the habit of creating something before you consume anything. For example, write that blog post before you watch YouTube videos. Earn the right to relax. Marie Forleo has a great vlog on this.

HEAD

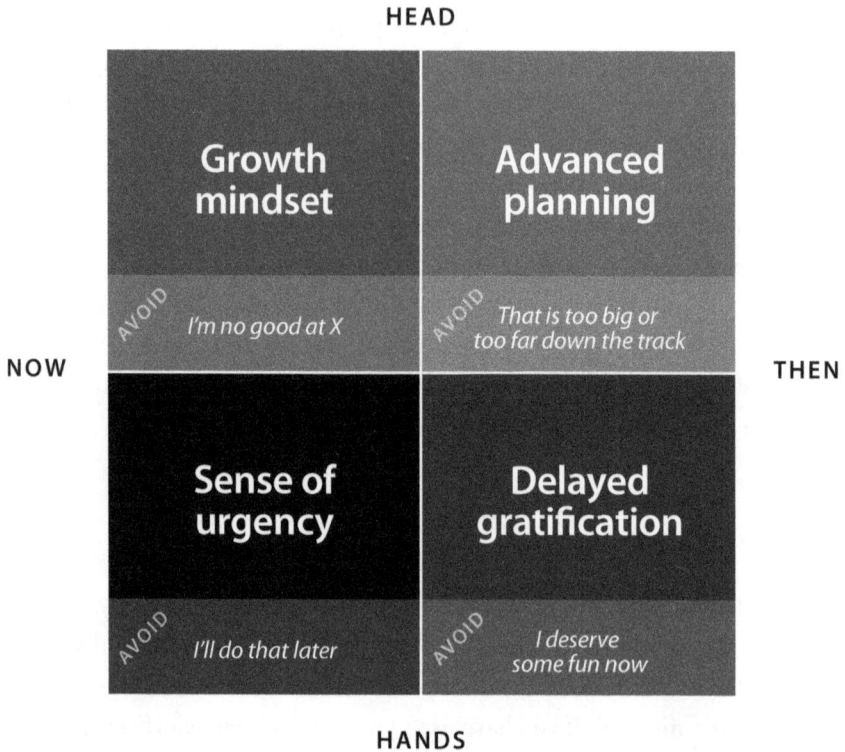

Growth
mindset

Advanced
planning

AVOID *I'm no good at X*

AVOID *That is too big or
too far down the track*

NOW

THEN

Sense of
urgency

Delayed
gratification

AVOID *I'll do that later*

AVOID *I deserve
some fun now*

HANDS

Figure 18. **Antidote to Inertia**

A Growth Mindset

Creation is also about your mindset. Carol Dweck's work on growth mindsets will help you to appreciate the difference between trying to be the best and getting better at something.

In her book *Mindset: The New Psychology of Success*, Dweck unpacks this idea in detail. A growth mindset focuses on getting better, rather than being the best. It says 'I can get better at anything,' resisting the mindset that says 'I am no good at X.'

Action precedes clarity.

At its heart, a growth mindset is the ethos of continuous improvement. Focussing less on the result and more on the process builds your resilience and your ability to succeed under pressure. Trevor Ragan from TrainUgly.com, a US-based basketball and volleyball coach, created a video that does a great job of summarising Dweck's research.

Delayed Gratification

In the pursuit of freedom, many people step back from taking responsibility for their lives. A hedonistic, entitled, 'I deserve this now' mind is immature and will stop you doing what you truly value. Being OK with the idea of gaining significant joy later is a core idea in the maturation of mankind.

The good news is that, in most cases, deferring small pleasures now for greater pleasures later, gets easier the longer you stick at it. It operates on the principle of compounding benefits. Investing now and focussing on the habits, not the result, means that in time, you will get better results than you could have imagined.

Advanced Planning

Getting unnecessary urgency out of your life is pretty simple. Pack the night before, review your week ahead on Sundays and prepare for stuff before you need to. All of this means that you have less real urgency.

Dr Stephen Covey taught that planning in advance is the first of the Seven Habits he attributes to highly successful people. It is the basis of the famous Important versus Urgent model. Goethe, the 17th-century German philosopher described the same idea, saying, 'Seldom should we let the urgent take the place of the important, and yet oftentimes we do!' American President and General Dwight Eisenhower used the same idea in his decision matrix. Preparing things before you need them is smart. The metaphor that you should dig your well before you are thirsty contains every motivation you need to buy into this habit.

Summary

Sometimes we just need help getting started. Success builds its own momentum, but getting off the ground can be hard. Generational unemployed have huge inertia issues to deal with, and we can all fall into the stuck state. Do the four things outlined in this chapter if you find yourself stuck in a rut they just might help you build some momentum.

ONLINE REFERENCES

Anderson, G. https://www.themodernnomad.com/
finding-vs-creating-yourself/

Eisenhower Matrix. https://www.eisenhower.me/eisenhower-matrix/

Forleo, M. When Getting Inspired Gets You In Trouble. https://www.youtube.com/watch?v=tMbhhR5I5gI

Four Minute Books. https://fourminutebooks.com/

LaBeouf, S., 2015. Just Do It. https://www.youtube.com/watch?v=ZXsQAXx_ao0

Martin, M., 2013. Speaker Showcase. https://www.youtube.com/watch?v=KK7JBaV7Zlc

Ragan, T. Train Ugly. https://www.youtube.com/watch?v=75GFzikmRY0

BOOKS MENTIONED

Cook, P., 2013. *The New Rules of Management: How to Revolutionise Productivity, Innovation and Engagement by Implementing Projects That Matter.* Australia: John Wiley and Sons. Australia.

Covey, S., 2013. *The 7 Habits of Highly Effective People: Powerful Lessons in Personal Change.* 25th Anniversary ed. United States: Simon & Schuster.

Dweck, C.S., 2016. *Mindset: The New Psychology of Success.* Updated ed. United States: Penguin Random House New York.

Ries, E., 2011. *The Lean Startup.* United States: Random House New York.

McGonigal, K., 2012. *The Willpower Instinct: How Self-Control Works, Why It Matters, and What You Can Do To Get More of It.* United States: Penguin Random House.

Tracy, B., 1984. *The Psychology of Achievement. Audio CD unabridged.* United States: Nightingale Conant.

QUESTIONS

1 Would you say you have a 'be the best' or a 'get better' mindset?

2 What positive thing could you start today that has no immediacy to it?

3 What will it take for you to do the biggest, toughest thing, first in your day?

4 What could you choose to say no to for now, so that you can say yes to something bigger down the track?

5 When under the pump, is there anything unusual you could let yourself do that might actually hack stress?

STATE MATTERS MORE THAN SCRIPT

Leadership is often viewed as the managing of scarce resource effectively. At other times it's expressed as the managing of what others do. Resourcefulness and world best practice have a part to play in success. The factor that is very much in the leadership zone, is the ability to choose who you are being as you lead. It turns out that people observe less what you say and more what you do. Or to be more accurate, who you are being while the doing happens. From this perspective, your personal state will matter way more than the scripts and dialogues you use as a leader.

I f I asked how you are feeling right now, could you tell me? Could you describe it in detached detail? Can you separate your sense of self from the energetic state you are experiencing? A key breakthrough moment for leaders is moving from experiencing a particular energy to observing the experience of that energy. That's a heavy sentence, I know. I had to take a moment to track its meaning, even as I wrote it.

There's a cliché that CEO stands for Chief Energy Officer. Whatever your leadership position, status or hierarchy in a business, you are at the centre of the energy that people experience in your company.

Knowing that you are experiencing a certain kind of energy gives you the ability to shift, to contemplate or leverage that energy. The moment that defines a person's rise into leadership is that point when they elect to be in a particular state, rather than be affected by it. You do get to choose your state.

When I tell you something about me, it's my truth. When I tell you something about you, it's an opinion.

The second moment of truth comes when you realise that your energetic choices also affect those around you. Whether you comprehend this from a mechanical or a metaphysical perspective, the result is the same. In a balanced physical state, we are unaffected by an endocrine inheritance. There, we get to choose how we feel, and that choice then affects how others feel. Maya Angelou said 'I've learned that people will forget what you said, people will forget what you did, but people will never forget how you made them feel.'

As a leader, your state matters more than your script.

Are you aware of your current state?

Can you choose a different state?

Can you read my energy and state?

Are you a slave to your state or master of it?

5	Leveraged	*Your presence enables others to move through these stages*
4	Effective	*You are able to exist effectively in all states and scenarios*
3	Efficient	*You develop the cabability to choose and authentically alter your state*
2	Powerless	*You are aware of your state but feel unable to affect it*
1	Oblivious	*You are completely unaware of your state and the impact it's having on others*

Figure 19. **Stage of State**

Once you start to read your energy, it then becomes a natural progression that you can start to read mine. A word of caution: we need to take care when reading the energy of others. Make sure that we are not projecting our state onto them, or misreading their state. With assumption being the mother of mistakes, take time to ask questions before making statements. It serves to remember the following when reading another person's energy. When I tell you something about me, it's my truth. When I tell you something about you, it's an opinion. Many people are unaware of their own state and may become confused and confronted by your seeing of them.

In leadership, state matters more than script. Who you are being, has a more significant impact on others than anything you say or do. While the sequence is not absolute, it might be useful to consider the process of awareness in the five stages on page 161.

So much focus, in the world and this book, is on you Rising Up to become the leader within. That shift into leadership works both ways – sometimes you need to go higher and sometimes you need to go deeper. Higher means vibrating at a higher energy level and putting down the petty squabbles of daily life. Going deeper is about finding a calm quiet place inside. Therein you find an infinite supply of energy, focus and clarity. A place for you, as a leader, to be in the world and meet whatever life chooses to put in front of you.

One way of looking at the deeper conversation is to ground yourself in the present moment. To feel deeply who you are, where you are, and what is happening around you. I know that the hour or day before a high stakes presentation, (and I believe they all are) I can easily get hyped. My adrenal system is on alert, my energy lifts and I do a run-through of what I might say or what may be useful for an audience. I have noticed that this anticipation can generate a disconnect between who I am being, what I am saying and what the audience needs at that moment. As a result, I know that I need to ground myself, so I've developed an awareness of strategies that help me to go deeper.

Here is a list of some that work for me, helping me to move in either direction as a leader. Don't take these as true for you or pre-scriptive, but figure out a few key ways that you can move up and down as required.

Higher

Sit still and go quiet.
When I need to elevate my state, my go-to is meditation. Develop the habit and make sitting quietly a key part of your routine. Morning and night, it will change your life. It's better than coffee – though I still love coffee! Beware, though, because you will soon realise that you are not the voice in your head. And once that happens, it's all over, and you will have no choice but to expand into your leadership potential.

DJ your life.
I find music is a tonic for my soul. Certain songs played at certain times, in a certain way can shift my energy super quick. Headphones are everywhere in my world, enabling me to tap into the power of music at any time. That means I can listen to what I want, when I need it, as loud as I want it. I use Spotify and YouTube heavily and have learned that one song on high rotation can help me manage my state. If interested, then you are welcome to follow me on YouTube, where I occasionally make playlists public. Although our tastes may be different, it's all about how music alters our state. There are some key moments where public music sets the stage for everyone.

Scan for short bursts of wisdom.
Not all books are created equal. My book *Next* focuses on how lead-ers lead in a decade of disruption. In the chapter, *Reading Reinvented*, I unpack some ways to hack your readership. The books that get me high have changed over time. It used to be that stories of heroes lifted me, then I discovered books that delved into different ways

of thinking. Nowadays, I read books that deliver wisdom and truth, whose purpose is to get me high. I love real books and read on a kindle with the app also on my phone. I often read a chapter before I meditate. If it's a good book, I read a page. If it's amazing, I read a paragraph and if it's an inspired piece of writing, I find one sentence is enough. One day it may take a single word. Find what you need based on where you are now. Be intentional about having these kinds of books only a moment away.

Laugh smart.

Well-constructed comedy is very powerful. Comedy is essentially the skill of recontextualising a situation. This is a key way to get some uplift. People get bogged down in the content of life, and being able to shift levels of abstraction unlocks the ability to Rise Up. Once again, it's about finding your funny, not mine. I like the American political satire of Stephen Colbert, John Oliver, Trevor Noah and Seth Myers. I suspect this is because of the secondary agenda around freedom of speech. You know you are in a fascist state if comedians can't poke fun at leaders. The filmmaker and cinematographer Albert Maysles once said, 'Tyranny is the deliberate removal of nuance.' I think this holds personally true as well. Laughter may be the best

> *The moment that defines a person's rise into leadership is that point when they elect to be in a particular state, rather than be affected by it.*

medicine, but it's also a gateway to higher states. Choose smart comedy so that you are forced to see ideas differently. The Netflix special Nanette by Hannah Gatsby might interest you, or Patriot Act by Hassan Minaj, also on Netflix.

Develop a Rise Squad.

There are certain people in my life with whom I connect with when I want to Rise Up. These are the people I will gladly talk to on a day of presentation, as I know they will leave me elevated. They believe in me, never bring fear into a conversation and through their attention, I get to see myself as the best version of myself. If you are indeed the sum total of the five people you spend the most time with, then you may want to get very intentional about who is in your squad. A word of caution, you may not, and probably won't, live with these people. It's hard to get a rise squad going when the daily grind of your life is present. I think many people start a journey of Rising Up and then start to exit or resent the core people in their life as they don't fit the new state. Personal development has a lot to answer for in this space. Sure, sometimes when you choose to live a higher life, you grow apart, but I suspect that you are looking for a rise in all the wrong places. It's OK if your rise squad is not at home.

Deeper

Be deeply present.
If meditation allows you to dissolve the sense of a separate self, then mindfulness allows you to make a profound connection with your world. Zen Buddhist Monk, Thích Nhất Hạnh (Master Thầy) teaches this beautifully. I like to think of mindfulness as being completely present. Master Thầy suggests you can do this while walking, sitting, eating, listening and speaking.

Dr Hawkins refers to this process of gently allowing and experiencing 'what is', as 'finessing the phenomena.' There is much to this idea. At its simplest level, grab a coffee, a tea or perhaps some unsalted mixed nuts. Sit with the item and eat or drink it as consciously as you can. Grind the brazil nut into a paste and note the texture on your tongue. Mindful consumption of anything you eat or drink can help you to become grounded.

Consume solids.
While I think that fasting can help you Rise Up, eating something substantial can equally ground you. It's as simple as sitting down and

having something to eat. Add in the prior mindfulness process, and you get a two for one. In the future, I might well choose a plant-based diet (I am one week in as this book goes to print), but when I feel like I need to ground myself, red meat works. I'll leave that choice to you. Quite simply, eating grounds you.

Connect to nature.

Nothing new or surprising here. Sit under a tree, take your shoes off, hug a tree or smell a flower. Grind your feet into the sand at the water's edge or roll pebbles in your hand. Take time to open up all your senses to the natural environment. Most built environments have small pockets of nature. Get good and locating these wherever where you are and use them to go deeper.

Hold or be held.

Physical contact can heal and ground you. It's extraordinary that many of us can live without touch for so long. While this suggestion has the chance to be misinterpreted, for me, it's simple. If I need to ground myself, physical contact helps. Book a massage, hug a friend, hold hands with someone. It's not for everyone, but big on my list.

Feel deeply.

A final idea is to feel into strong emotion, rather than avoid it. Sit with the feeling, immerse yourself in it without losing yourself to it. Allow it to fill your consciousness. Feelings are not permanent, nor are they real, yet feeling deeply enables you to go both up and down. Observe the feeling as something that occurs for you, not to you. If you can achieve this, you get to run experiential movies each starring a strong emotion. As with physical contact, this is not for everyone, and perhaps not the first thing to try. For me, though, it is a powerful way to manage state.

So, go ahead and Rise Up, but at the same time make sure you have your feet on the ground. That doesn't have to mean you are stuck, so lift a little. Rise Up.

ONLINE REFERENCES

Church, M., https://www.youtube.com/channel/
UCY2A00uUS5yIQp6hIEXhUOA

BOOKS MENTIONED

Church, M., 2017. *Next*. Australia: Thought Leaders Publishing.

Hawkins, D., 2001. *The Eye of the I: From Which Nothing is Hidden*. United States: Veritas Publishing.

QUESTIONS

1 Are you aware of your current state?

_____

_____

_____

2 Can you choose a different state?

_____

_____

_____

3 Can you read another's energy and state?

_____

_____

_____

4 Are you the slave or master of your state at work? At home?

_____

_____

_____

5 What are your go-to state management strategies?

_____

_____

_____

16

PEACE AT WORK, PEACE IN THE WORLD

Composure comes from internal peace. Leaders who can create calm within chaos are rare indeed and highly prized. This chapter explores the idea of calm as a contagious quality that drives safety and security through a group of people. One of the indicators that a leader is highly evolved is their ability to keep their head when others are losing theirs. This chapter explores the three roles of a leader and the effective way to manage the perception of threats.

The Rise is often satirically referred to as rah-rah or hype. Enthusiastic, confident leaders can quickly be discounted if their enthusiasm lacks a certain composure and gentle vulnerability. It's as if their pumped-up nature is not the whole story, and lacks authenticity.

'The subtle aggression of personal development' is a turn of phrase that Melbourne-based psychologist Bob Sharples shares in his writings, speaking to our intuitive distrust of the push for more. It's a lovely phrase, so rich in the truth of how unkind we can be to ourselves on the journey to self-improvement. The self-help movement can often have an assumption of 'not good enough', and its sales process is typically one of gap analysis.

In an attempt to sell us something, a need or want that we apparently lack is identified or created so that the vendor can satisfy or fix a perceived gap. So many of the things we own are a result of need fabricated out of an assumed lack.

In this book, it's my goal to soften the aggressive, 'There is something wrong with you' approach, and present ideas on personal growth, within the leadership context, in a way that redefines self-development. Moving from a paradigm of 'You are not enough' to 'You have everything you need within you.' I think this creates better leaders who go onto generate further better leaders. We need to ensure that our leadership does not harm others and perhaps even more critically, does no harm to ourselves. Leaders who Rise Up, do so with humility, grace and calm, ensuring that they first do no harm.

In the martial art Aikido, there is a goal of mastery. It is the metaphor of walking through a battlefield, hurting no one and being hurt by no one. For me, this journey occurs in three stages:

1. You begin with the ability to defend yourself by hurting others.

2. Next, it's protecting others without getting yourself hurt.

3. Eventually, though, the pursuit of mastery in martial arts shifts metaphors and you simply stop fighting.

Any martial artist who maintains the pursuit of mastery will come close to this final lesson. They have learnt to fight so that they never have to.

I think the vulnerability journey is similar:

1. First, you protect yourself by building
   a seemingly strong identity.

2. Next, you start to shift the focus from 'self' to
   'others.' You drop your guard, confident that
   you can judge who is safe and who is not.

3. You soon realise that there is no reason
   to have any guard at all.

Each stage is self-fulfilling. When you see everyone as a threat, you attract fights. When you see everyone as dangerous, you get hurt. When you begin to separate people into those you can trust and those you can't, you create competition and politics. But when you can exist without judging others, you are truly open. Perhaps openness is another word for vulnerability.

> *Leaders who Rise Up, do so with humility, grace and calm, ensuring that they first do no harm.*

The word 'vulnerable' is not very accessible in a commercial space and not easy for leaders to grasp. In her seminars and books, Dr Brené Brown explains why it matters. Her book, *Daring Greatly: How the courage to be vulnerable transforms the way we live* is entirely on this message. The standard definition of vulnerable though, is being *exposed to the possibility of being attacked or harmed, either physically or emotionally, i.e. 'We were in a vulnerable position.'* A synonym search for the word says that to be vulnerable is to be *in danger, in peril, in jeopardy, at risk, endangered, unsafe, unprotected, ill-protected, unguarded.* Perhaps *unguarded* is closest in meaning here.

For a leader to be so, they need to hear *vulnerable* in the right way. This is a classic above the line distinction and a question of perspective. Below the line, it means exposed to attack. Above the line, however, there is no attack, and so there is no risk. When you feel that the world is out to get you, being vulnerable is a dangerous thing. When you feel that the world is you, you are free to access the power of being open.

The concept of being a vulnerable leader is often in conflict with being a strong leader in times of disruption and uncertainty. Some global politicians, both historically and currently are anything but open, vulnerable and authentic. They were elected or allowed to take power because a large number of people were scared and craved the perceived promise of strength. They failed to recognise the masquerade of belligerence and ignorance. As Lord Acton said 'Power corrupts and absolute power corrupts absolutely'. He went on to say that 'All great men are bad men,' but I'll let you get distracted by his Wikipedia page. It raises the question of whether a strong leader can also be a vulnerable one. Thích Nhất Hạnh often says that 'The stronger you are, the gentler you become.' In other words, true strength is gentle. Gentle on yourself, gentle on others and gentle on the situation. When you are gentle, you demonstrate composure, and composure is contagious.

Composure is something I wish I had more of.

I like to think of myself as a steady, at ease, man. One you can rely on to keep his head when everyone else is losing theirs. Yet my wish to be that calm person is not always how I have shown up. I get scared, I say the wrong thing, I put pressure on when I shouldn't, and I do let other's stress response affect me – sometimes.

But not all the time, and that's the point.

'Leadership calm' is a learned skill. It's not the absence of fear and stress; it's exercising the right to choose your response in a given set of circumstances. To be useful in moments of stress, we want our leaders to help us manage our fear, remove our confusion, and keep us moving towards a better future.

One of my dearest and oldest friends, Mark Dobson, is currently the Sydney critical incident manager for Team Rubicon. Mark is one calm cat and I have seen him lead in some significant crises. Team Rubicon is a very cool organisation, founded by two retired, United States servicemen – a marine sniper and an intelligence officer. Jake Wood, the CEO and founder, realised that soldiers had a particular skill-set that should continue to be utilised post-retirement. Team Rubicon focuses on serving vulnerable and at-risk populations affected by a disaster. The Team Rubicon story is moving; check them out on YouTube.

When you are gentle, you demonstrate composure, and composure is contagious.

I love the simplicity and playfulness of Team Rubicon's rules of engagement. 'Don't be a dick' is their first rule, and the essence of it is to stay calm under crisis. Jake Wood talks about it all over the web and former Navy SEAL Commander, Rorke Denver, explains the mantra in his talk. 'Calm is contagious,' he says. 'Especially when that calm is coming from the man or woman in charge. If the men begin to lose their wits, if the group is unsure of what to do next, it's the leader's job to do one thing: instil calm – not by force, but by example.' You don't have to feel calm yourself as a leader; sometimes, you just have to act calm.

That's who you want to be, whatever your line of work; the casual, relaxed person in every situation who tells everyone else to take a breath and not to worry, because 'you've got this'. Don't be the agitator, the paranoid, the worrier, or the irrational. Be the calm person, not the liability. It will catch on.

You've got this...

So for me, there are three tones we can use more often as leaders:

1. Remove fear and replace it with confidence by telling your people, 'You've got this', and if you are on the front line with them, about to face down a challenge then 'We've got this'.

2. Remove the confusion and replace it with certainty. Use phrases like 'One step at a time', 'Trust the process', 'Stay the course', and let people know what the next best action is. It turns out any action will often do, as culture is more powerful than strategy.

3. Mobilise us all in pursuit of a better future. Use words like 'onwards' and 'next'. The job of a leader is to help manage the overload of stressful times. Focus on what we need to do now, what we need to do next, and eventually what we need to do in a future then. Now, Next and Then; three time horizons that are useful in times of stress. Leaders triage the priorities for the rest of us so that we can have courage and take action in the presence of fear.

Composure creates the space for genuine connection, or what might be called intimacy. It is something we crave, something we hide from, something we fall deeply for and for me it's a never-ending life lesson. Phonetically, we can break the word intimacy down into the phrase *'into me I see.'* This is true, as intimacy with others is only part of the story. It is essential to be intimate within ourselves. As a leader, being vulnerable is knowing yourself so intimately that you have a secure sense of self. It's what many life schools call Self with a capital 'S'.

Your job as a leader is to inspire confidence. Yet your relationship with those you lead may demand a depth of intimacy, which leaves you feeling exposed as a leader and at risk. For many, the only way they experience intimacy is through the mutual exchange of secrets with the leader. Tantamount to salacious gossip, this special access to your dreams and fears is how this type of person forms intimacy with you. It raises a question, though, around what it takes to be intimate with another in a leadership context. Is it the sharing of secrets, exposing of weakness, is it about allowing drama and gossip to direct the relationship? And is this something you, as a leader, should pursue?

My answer is no this is not what being open means. Sure be open to the moment, the experience of the Now. But don't open yourself up to the little love that creates a bond at the expense of someone else. This is akin to sex equals intimacy or drugs equal enlightenment, gossip approximates intimacy. But it is not it. Watch your teams for gossip, sarcasm, jargon or cynicism: these are the four horsemen of toxic tribes. Leaders inspire us, not just with their vision of what we should be doing, but also through their example. You don't have to find drama or secrets or express your inner fears to achieve the intimacy that is often confused with open, authentic leadership.

Summary

Be gentle as you rise, gentle on others and yourself. It's easier to be vulnerable when you operate from above the line. Calm is contagious and creates a space for leadership intimacy to go to work.

ONLINE REFERENCES

Denver, R., 2015. https://www.youtube.com/watch?v=i5Clwch7meU

Team Rubicon. https://www.youtube.com/user/teamrubiconusa

Wikipedia contributors. (2019, August 1). John Dalberg-Acton, 1st Baron Acton. In Wikipedia, The Free Encyclopedia. https://en.wikipedia.org/wiki/John_Dalberg-Acton,_1st_Baron_Acton

BOOKS MENTIONED

Brown, B., 2012. *Daring Greatly: How the courage to be vulnerable transforms the way we live.* United States: Penguin Random House.

Sharples, B. 2012. *Meditation and Relaxation in Plain English.* United States: Wisdom Publications.

QUESTIONS

1 What meaning do you attach to the word vulnerable?

_____
_____
_____

2 How safe is it to be you at work?

_____
_____
_____

3 How safe is it to be you at home?

_____
_____
_____

4 How calm are you during crisis, and what can you do to be more so?

_____
_____
_____

5 Can you recall a leader with composure, what did that do for you as someone who worked/lived with them?

_____
_____
_____

LEADERSHIP AWARENESS

In essence, this entire book is a project to raise the awareness of those who want to lead and influence. This chapter gets to the heart of that awareness and provides a discriminatory model for some rudimentary distinctions between levels. Read this chapter lightly, it goes from a concrete view of the world to a very abstract one quite quickly. Just get the bit you need, based on the level you can access and utilise right now. The rest will sit like seeds and may take root just when you need the wisdom of a different level of awareness. Rise Up and bring others up with you.

How aware are you of different perspectives?

This question is critical for leadership in the decade of disruption. Leaders, today, need to excel in three campaigns. The race to the future (innovation and adaptability), the war for talent (engagement and productivity) and the battle for attention (differentiation and positioning). Your consciousness as a leader becomes critical in a world of growing complexity. Silo-ing is a result of a lack of awareness. Low Net Promoter Scores, poor engagement and disrupted cultures are the products of inadequate leadership and team awareness. Awareness in the leadership body makes everything better across the whole organisation.

So how do you develop your awareness and that of your team? This is hard work as you can only teach, instruct, or lead to your own level of understanding.

Can you rise above the noise of an experience? Are you able to see what is going on around you? Or are you stuck in one perspective? You can only be effective within a set viewpoint if things around you stay the same. For many years this was the case in business, as the operating context for a product or service was fairly contained and stable. Of course, in a volatile, unpredictable, complex and ambiguous marketplace, the rigid reliability of a certain industry or sector is less certain.

When we forgive, we don't necessarily condone another's behaviour. Equally, when we tune in, we don't necessarily agree with the collective conversation.

One of the ways leaders help us with the race to the future is by being agile and encouraging new perspectives. Incidentally, this is one of the primary commercial justifications for an assertive diversity and inclusion agenda. Einstein's mantra that you cannot solve a problem with the level of thinking that created it speaks to this.

7	Primary Question	*What would love do?*
6	Deep Truth	*What do you know to be true?*
5	Considered Response	*What is new or possible?*
4	Group Energy	*What is the group vibe?*
3	Thematic Drive	*What is it actually about?*
2	Meaning Made	*What do you make that mean?*
1	Stuff of Life	*What actually happened?*

Figure 20. The Seven Levels of Leadership Awareness

Leaders who are fixed in their perspectives tend to become ineffective once the game shifts around them. And like putting your feet in a stream, today's work environment is always changing. The river is the same, but the water rushing by is different at any moment.

This chapter explores seven levels of leadership awareness as I see them.

Understanding these levels is the first step. You can only lead your team or enterprise to the level of your awareness and each business unit is limited by a lack of understanding about their operating level. It's about seeing what is going on and, as a result, not being at the effect of it.

Step two is about improving the peripheral vision of your key people so that they become better at surfing the edges of their own understanding. Greater awareness creates space for leaders to hold events and experiences lightly. It enables them to maintain composure in the face of chaos, to be the voice of progress and ultimately be the space for what is happening. The meta-question then, is 'Can I be the space for the Is-ness of this moment?'

LEVEL ONE: (CONTENT)

The Stuff of Life: *What are we perceiving?*

This is where all the drama—the good and the bad—exists. For many people this *is* life, and their world view is 'I live, I eat, I sit; repeat.' Leaders need to stay connected to this level of awareness as it is the reality for many people they work with. Leaders need to anchor their ideas with living example in the form of stories and by providing numeric evidence. When you listen to another, respond to their stuff, their content. Don't just appear to listen while waiting for your turn to speak. Listen to what is said, and avoid reacting to it. Keep your stuff out of it.

The Meaning Made:
What have we made that mean?

Humans are meaning-making machines, and there is a massive risk of assumption, making an ass out of u and me. The easiest way to understand the meaning that someone is making is to ask. 'So when you say BLAH, do you mean X or something else?' Equally, when you are sharing a story, a case study or a set of numbers, be explicit and upfront about the lens through which you are sharing the information. In the absence of a declared meaning, we will make one up. If you are receiving a message, don't. If you are sharing a message, be sure to establish the point early and frequently.

The Thematic Drive: *What is that actually about?*

The final level of functional, designed awareness is context. In terms of leadership awareness, this means the highest abstraction of an idea. If Level One explored what is said, and Level Two delved into what is meant, then Level Three unpacks what it's actually about. This awareness is through the lens of sense-making. In simplest terms, whoever commands the context controls the conversation. A leader makes sure they are intentional about establishing and managing this level of awareness.

A note on Pink Sheets

One of the ideas that is the backbone of what we do at Thought Leaders, is teaching people to capture, package and deliver their ideas through the lens of these first three levels. Understanding that what you say makes a point and sits within a bigger theme is key to clever people being commercially smart. We call this thinking process, the Pink Sheet. I wrote a book on that which you can download and read, plus a series of educational videos about the process. You can discover more at pinksheetprocess.com.

The Group Energy:
What is the group vibe right now?

The Germans have a word for the prevailing mood of a time, Zeitgeist. As you are reading this, there will be a predominant conversation happening in society. Depending on where you get your inputs from, it might be what your friends are discussing, it might be what is in the news (heaven forbid) or perhaps what is trending on social media. As I write this, Trump is being impeached, people are identifying as non-binary, and the Middle East is a mess. Getting tuned into the collective tone, the social memes and the narrative of vocal influencers is a smart leadership strategy.

I love the distinction that when we forgive, we don't necessarily condone another's behaviour. Equally, when we tune in, we don't necessarily agree with the collective conversation. Anthropologist Margaret Mead said, 'Never underestimate the power of a small group of dedicated people to change the world; indeed it's the only thing that ever has.' The civil rights movement is a perfect case in point. Fighting against the prevailing mood is often the right choice and running counter to a market place is often commercially smart. But be sure that in doing so, you are clearly aware of how the game is being played.

The Considered Response: *What is new or possible, what is our best response?*

Awareness gives you a chance to respond. Victor Frankl in his book *Man's Search for Meaning* states that 'Everything can be taken from a man but one thing: the last of human freedoms – to choose one's attitude in any given set of circumstances, to choose one's own way.' The point of awareness is that we get to do something with it. Perhaps you want to ask your team what they wish to do with a particular idea. What does history expect of us? What does our customer want of us? What do our values ask us to do? What does the future require of us? What does the board need from us? What is the essential reaction? What is new or possible? What is our best response? Thinking through different options and scenarios creates new possibilities. Breaking the status quo and opens up new futures.

The Deep Truth: *What do we know to be absolutely true? What are the relative truths that support dogma and thus reduce liberty?*

What is true? As a leader, it's worth asking the question 'What do we know to be true in this situation?' What I like about level six, is that you get to explore what is actually true, versus what is considered to be true. Challenging existing mindsets can be confronting. Declaring 'Here is a dangerous idea!' offers license to explore the edges of what is considered sacrosanct. It gives oxygen to people's intuitive knowing in a world that is heavily reliant on provable evidence. Exploring relative truths creates its own elevation in awareness. The act itself opens your mind. What is valid for one person at one time in life may not be true for all people at that time. Exploring the fluidity of people's relative truth helps a leader overcome personal bias and, at the same time, expand the consciousness of the team. What do you know to be true?

The Interbeing Question:
Who am I being in all this?

Zen Buddhists create Koans or word puzzles designed to disengage thinking and push awareness to new levels. One such question, or Koan, is 'what was your face before your parents were born?' or 'What am I?' as opposed to 'Who am I?' Interbeing is the Buddhist concept of 'the me in you' or the fact that everything is made up of non-thing elements. A flower is composed of sun, water and soil elements and as such the flower interbe's with all its component non-flower elements. The conceptual equivalent is to act as if every experience you are having is part of who you are. It leads to the question, 'If I am in you and you are in me, then how does what's happening right now serve me?' Act as if you have created what you are observing and then ask 'How does this serve me?' In so doing, you may reveal new levels of awareness.

Summary

Leadership has three critical demands on it: the first being the ability to take fear and replace it with confidence, the second being to remove confusion and put certainty in its place, and the third being to mobilise us in pursuit of a better future. Meeting these three demands is increasingly difficult in the age of uncertainty. Leaders have to make decisions in a fast-paced world, often without all the facts. And they do so in an environment of increasing complexity. You can counter these challenges by expanding your awareness as a leadership group.

ONLINE REFERENCES

Pink Sheets. pinksheetprocess.com

BOOKS MENTIONED

Frankl, Viktor E. 1984. *Man's search for meaning: an introduction to logotherapy.* New York: Simon & Schuster.

QUESTIONS

1 When you listen to others, can you separate what they are saying and what they mean?

_____

_____

_____

2 Are you able to then determine what that is actually about?

_____

_____

_____

3 Can you give a one word theme (context) to describe a movie you like?

_____

_____

_____

4 Think back on a conversation or meeting you had recently, was your response from love or something else?

_____

_____

_____

5 If love was not the response that time, how might your response be different next time?

_____

_____

_____

MANAGING WITH KINDNESS

Managing people has a certain brutality to it in the commercial world. The economic model makes workers the cost of production, and production the God. Economic theories aside, the war for talent means a human-centred leadership approach will return culture and performance gains. As more and more of the process of production is automated, it's the creative application that will become more highly valued. The focus of this chapter is engaging, mentoring and developing people so that they experience joy, satisfaction and a freshness through your leadership.

When you see someone doing something you don't like, or that triggers you, run towards them, not away.

The key phrase I was taught is, 'just like me.' If someone cuts you off in traffic, you might put psychological distance between them and you by getting angry. Or you might recall a time when you were the other person, in a hurry and driving selfishly, being self-serving. You realise the other driver is 'just like me'. Seeing the world as 'us and them' is the small game; playing 'just like me' means you begin to play the bigger game. The bigger game is the leadership game. It's the game of love. This is why win-lose negotiating is a thing of the past, and why it's so surprising to still stumble across it in daily life. It's hard to imagine living in that constant state of fear, thinking 'the world is out to get me, so I better get my share first'.

In a similar vein, it's easy to think that all the above the line, love stuff, means you never deal with problems. Many of the energy coaching gurus will tell you that often the higher you rise up, the greater the challenges presented. This is certainly true when you are working with other people. When you lead others, there will be some team members who need very little guidance, and others who need a great deal of your help to be the best version of themselves at work. This chapter examines how to manage team members who drop the ball *and* those who run with it.

In an ideal world, all team members would run with the ball all of the time. But that's rarely the case. We all drop the ball from time to time. The trick is figuring out the best way to handle it when it happens to one of your team.

The easiest way to manage a great team is to start with a group of high performers who all embrace best practice work and life strategies. At Thought Leaders, my business partner Peter Cook and I have created what we call our high-performance team framework (see page 195). It's brilliant when people run with the ball and bring their best to work:

The model is in two halves. The top represents what the business needs from high performers – things like respect, honesty, and

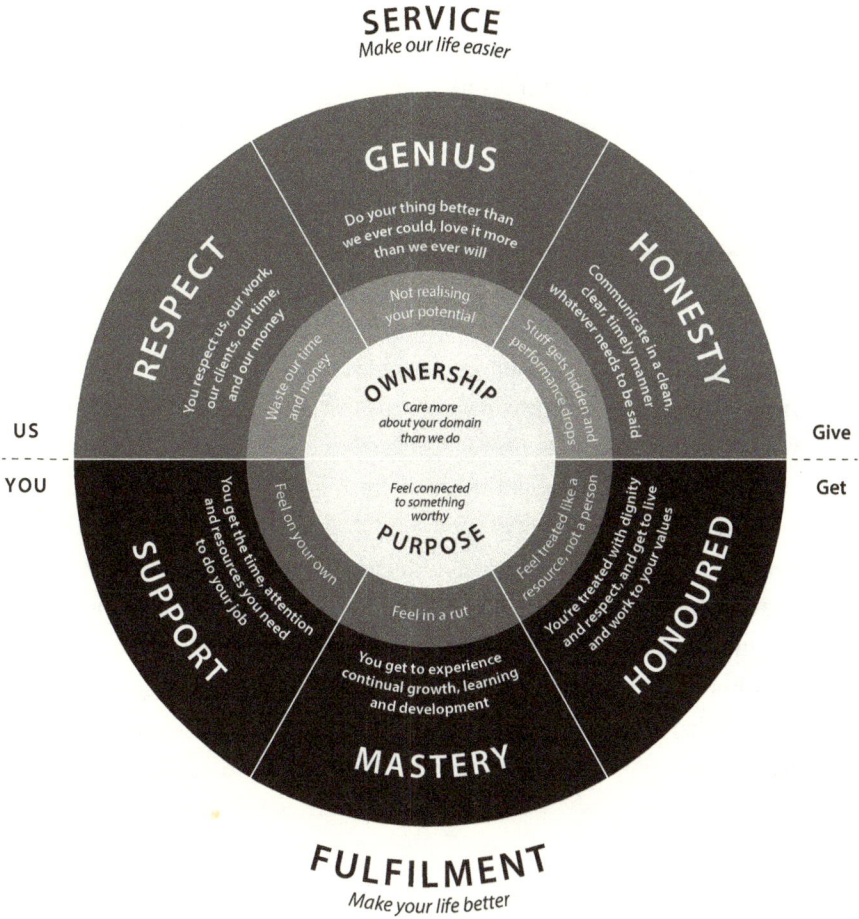

Figure 21. **Thought Leaders
High Performance Team Framework**

making best use of your genius. We call this 'making our life easier' or *service*.

The bottom half represents what the team member gets when working in this way – things like support, mastery, and the dignity and honour of being a unique person in the team. We call this 'making your life better' or *fulfilment*.

The model acts as an aspirational guide, and we use it to remind us of the ideals that we should all be striving to achieve every day. But it's not our daily reality.

We all drop the ball. When a team member is not operating at their best, it can get difficult to stay above the line. Sometimes they need coaching, sometimes they need mentoring, and sometimes they need to be confronted to prevent them from undermining the efforts of the whole team. We call this the Performance Intervention Guide (see page 197). While this is not a hard and fast, one-system-fits-all, it's used to guide our management team on when and how to intervene when they are trying to stay above the line themselves, but those around them are not.

This model details a variety of recommended strategies and actions that leaders or managers can take to respond to issues that a team member may have. The grid structure serves to guide our way of approaching performance issues differently, as various behaviours and personalities often require very different strategies to be effective.

The bigger game is the leadership game. It's the game of love.

A range of symptoms show managers where friction is occurring among team members and guide the appropriate dialogue to remedy it. You could use the model as an intervention map to help you better manage the performance of your teams so that high performers stay motivated and those performing poorly can be brought back on board.

EASE
Runner *Gives us energy* `SHIELD`

- Anticipates questions
- Removes friction
- Manages managers
- Updates, not requests

Take care of yourself
*'Anything you need?
Any battles I can fight?'*

WORK
Absent Busy *Costs us energy* `MENTOR`

- Inconsistent performance
- Great starter / poor finisher
- Communication blackspots
- Decreased responsibility and ownership

Manage your projects
'Don't make us bring it up first'

WORRY
Dropping balls *Erratic energy* `TRIAGE`

- Easily distracted
- Always busy
- Missing deadlines
- Enthusiastic in discussions about new things

Manage your priorities
'Do the important stuff first'

CANCER
Pushing back *Wrong energy* `COACH`

- That's not my job
- Making excuses
- Questions as stalling
- Bully others

Put yourself out
'Do what is asked of you first'

WEIGHT
Casually Passive *Provides no energy* `TEACH`

- Not taking notes in meetings
- Asking co-worker or manager versus looking for answer first
- Body present, mind absent

Start paying attention
*'Don't make us ask you
to do it twice'*

TOXIC
Deliberately Undermining *Saps team's energy* `CONFRONT`

- Sarcasm, gossip, cynicism
- Brings down morale
- Passive aggressive meetings

Get on board
*'Don't drag us all down
to your level'*

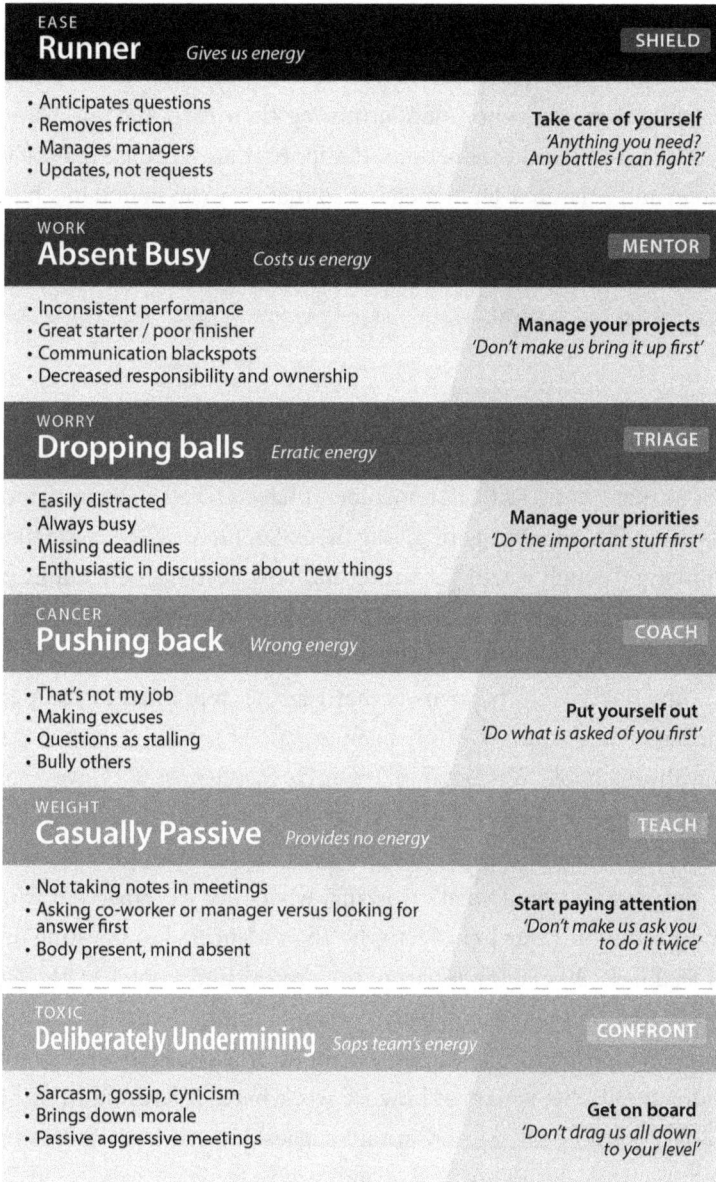

Figure 22. **Performance Intervention Guide**

Adjust your management response so that it is tailored to each issue on its own merits. In some instances, this may involve confronting someone who is undermining their own and the team's performance. In other situations, the appropriate response may be to shield and reassure a team member so that they can maintain a high level of performance. At its essence, you are trying to catch people doing the right things, and helping them when they are doing things that are less than ideal.

The disappointment trap

For as many years as I can remember, I have sucked at performance reviews. Either receiving or giving them. So, I have spent some time thinking through what I get wrong and how I can get better at helping others be the best version of themselves, and helping myself be open to doing something a better way.

Invariably what happens is that I get disappointed in the performance of a member of my team and don't handle it in the right way. In his book, *The Speed of Trust*, Dr Stephen M. R. Covey, son of the late great Dr S. R. Covey, states that for feedback to work, you need a 'cadence of accountability.' For example, every Monday have a conversation about what's working, what's not working, and what you need to do your job effectively. The cadence takes the sting out of feedback. By making it part of the process and system of managing others, you take the negative personal impact out of giving and receiving feedback. It becomes less about 'what you did wrong,' and more about 'this is part of how we work here.' Interestingly, in his book *Creativity Inc*, Steve Catmull suggests that a leading creative culture needs the ability to give and receive feedback to succeed, he calls it 'creative abrasion.'

Stanford University Professor, Robert Sutton, author of *Good Boss, Bad Boss*, uses the term *bosshole* to describe leaders who contribute to workplace negativity. The key point he makes is that the moment you express disappointment in someone you lead or manage is precisely when you stop leading. This is a big idea and at the heart of your intent around performance management. When someone lets you down, what do you do? Do you express disappointment in the hope that they improve their results, or do you respond with kindness?

Typically, things always start out well.

1. You see talent and engage with it.

2. The potential performance of that talent creates an expectation.

3. That expectation is either met or not. At some point, as the goalposts move and performance expectations exceed the 'moment in time' capability, you get the leadership 'moment of truth'.

At that moment, you can either express disappointment or respond with kindness.

The typical response is to have a *difficult conversation* within a performance review construct, and deliver some tough feedback.

In a classic Karpman drama triangle response, you might Blame, Bully or Rescue the relationship. The Blame: 'You have let the team down.' The Bully: 'Why can't you get this right? It's your F#$%ing job.' And the Rescuer: 'Fine, I will just do it myself.'

You can either express disappointment or respond with kindness.

Yet the three ideal responses in that moment of truth are kindness, encouragement and wisdom. The Kindness response: 'Are you OK? Anything going on that you need help with?' The Encouragement response: 'You've got this. I know you can make it work.' And the Wisdom response: 'Something to think about that might help is___.'

When you are below the line everyone annoys you, lets you down and is actively sabotaging you. Carl Jung wrote that 'Everything that irritates us about others can lead to an understanding of ourselves.'

The moment you are disappointed in someone else, stop and check yourself. This could be a moment to practice leading with kindness. Typically, extreme negative emotions like anger, sadness, fear and guilt are driven by some held or repressed feeling. Paradoxically cleaning up your own stuff helps you become better at attention out, and helps you lead above the line.

Everyone has good and bad days, whether they are the best performing veteran or the newest team member with the lowest confidence levels. The key point to recognise is that at certain times, they both need appropriate leadership and guidance to keep your team working above the line.

BOOKS MENTIONED

Catmull, S., & Wallace, A., 2014. *Creativity, Inc.: overcoming the unseen forces that stand in the way of true inspiration*. United States: Random House.

Covey, S. M. R., 2006. *The Speed of Trust: the one thing that changes everything*. United States: Simon & Schuster.

Sutton, R., 2010. *Good Boss, Bad Boss: How to Be the Best... and Learn from the Worst*. United States: Hachette Book Group.

QUESTIONS

1 If you drew your own high-performance model, what would be the six variables you would identify as key?

_____

_____

_____

2 Looking at the performance intervention guide, can you position key people at different levels on the guide?

_____

_____

_____

3 How do you currently manage disappointment?

_____

_____

_____

4 Is there any opportunity to practice kindness?

_____

_____

_____

5 Can you recognise the three responses of bully, blame and rescue in your management style?

_____

_____

_____

HOLDING HANDS

This chapter is bringing the people leadership qualities to a head by exploring how leaders either increase or decrease the threat of violence in a business. This may seem like a strange chapter to almost close on. The point is to provide you a time capsule for the moments when your evolution as a leader unearths fears and behaviours in and around you. These reactions will seem far from the intention you shaped and formed throughout your reading of this book. It's OK. The higher you go, the more intense the awareness becomes, and the darker some of the stuff that comes up. Watch for the violence of the knife of separation.

R
elationships are something else, aren't they? It's as if the emotional contracts we have with each other serve to stretch us and make us grow. I have two friends, committed soul mates who have an operating agreement that they will hold hands while arguing. I doubt they disagree much, but the idea is that if they do, it is never from a position of separation. They are 'one behind the two' and the holding of hands is the symbolic gesture that affirms this. Powerful stuff.

A leader rarely operates in a vacuum; at some point, you will have to deal with people. With this as a truism, I thought it might be useful to talk about the little acts of violence we use in our relationships that sever the connection we have with each other. These are often unconscious acts, and as Jung said, *'Until we make the unconscious conscious, it will direct our life, and we will call it fate.'*

Caroline Myss wrote a book titled *Sacred Contracts*. When my sister died, I found great solace in the premise that we form a relationship contract pre-birth and then get to experience our life and relationships as a series of life lessons. Lessons that play out on the stage of our life, where people we meet act as a cast of characters all in service of our soul's big mission. Now, before you get all 'paradigmy' on me, you don't have to buy into this as truth for the metaphor to be useful.

Stay with me.

If you could entertain this as a possibility, then it might be useful as a perspective that liberates you from feeling done unto by others. It fixes the victim mindset super-fast. Imagine that at some level, once upon a time, you chose to live in the relationship that hurts you right now. And that you did so to learn something.

What is that something?

What are you learning from that *shitty* husband, *crappy* parent, *messed up* business partner? If you can get the learning, then it's possible that the relationship shifts. This perspective is how you can stay in the seemingly untenable and grow from it. Indeed, perhaps you get to create something beautiful with the apparent suffering. As the Buddhists say, *no mud, no lotus*. Because as it turns out, at least in my world view, there is no such thing as a shitty husband, a crappy parent or a messed up anyone. It's all a reflection of the shitty, crappy, messed up experience or energy within you. Ask yourself, 'What do I need to learn right now, from this situation?' Get the learning, integrate it and move on. Together or apart becomes less important when you have learned or are learning, everything you can out of the contract.

Wayne Dyer once said that '*A relationship based on obligation has no grace*'. I shudder when I hear people say that relationships are all about compromise. They don't have to be. If you are learning, stay. If the learning is done, move on. No need to be violent about it, no need to be pushy or pully about it. It's pretty simple; learn or not learn. Grow or not grow.

The much-maligned 'conscious uncoupling' of Chris Martin and Gwyneth Paltrow, privileged though their life may be, seems to speak to this as a possibility. I get it, a darkly violent, abusive relationship, without the millions of dollars to consciously uncouple, may find it hard to receive any relevance from yet another celebrity break up. But just maybe, Chris and Gwyneth's publicly lived experience is an example of human 2.0 and next-level relationships. I choose to see it that way and thank them for modelling something graceful. It takes courage to put your life on the world stage for others to pick to pieces.

> *If you are learning, stay. If the learning is done, move on.*

From my privileged position, the key in all this relationship stuff is to remove the weapons and the violence. The worst acts of violence are the ones you don't see as such. Physical acts of domestic abuse leave horrible marks that show. The emotional ones do not, and that can make them hard to find and perhaps harder to face. I was discussing this chapter with a father at basketball last night (as you do?)

and he thought that denying your anger was a recipe for disaster. We discussed game theory and other processes used in therapy and anger management.

Historically any significant social change typically followed an act of violence. Protestors and activist certainly believe that sometimes an act of defiance and an act of violence are the same thing. Read a bit about monks who self-immolate, and the issue deepens. I believe that violence, of all types, is not helpful. So for me as much as possible I choose no more acts of violence. The small acts of violence that play out in personal relationships act as a knife of separation, breaking down the *us* and *we* that is implicit in any leadership endeavour.

When I judge you as wrong or not good enough, I am judging some part of me that has the same energy.

The wounds we leave on each other's souls cut the deepest. Denying others anything is how you most hurt the soul. You cannot shine the light on another's path without illuminating your own, and the reverse is true. Free the people in your life from expectations that they are required to be anyone to you, or do anything for you. It's your life, and it's their life. Stop fidget spinning with others' lives, clean up your stuff and choose to be free. No-one needs to get hurt in your pursuit of freedom. As you Rise Up as a leader, some will come with you, and some won't. That's OK, you do you.

My business partner, Peter Cook, has taken a vow of non-violence, which inspired me. (Just quietly, I decided that I could do the same without the whole ceremony, fasting, meditating and pledging.) It's funny, though, how subtle our acts of violence are and how the knife of separation, being the ultimate act of violence cuts both ways. When I judge you as wrong or not good enough, I am judging some part of me that has the same energy. Those who don't trust others don't trust themselves.

Until you have self-love, you can't have other-love. Until your other-love has no conditions, you can't experience what my friend and personal development guru, Lisa O'Neill, describes as Big Love.

There are three ways I notice that I have cut myself off from others:

Swearing

I know it's only a little thing, but when I swear, historically it's been to judge and hurt others. My 'F*#k off' is literal and has violence in it as opposed to 'Off you f*#k' that you utter to an annoying seagull at the beach. It's the intent, not the weapon that harms.

Judging

Whenever I find myself with an opinion that another is not enough in some way, I am committing an act of violence. I have found it's far more helpful to accept others as just like you, rather than a failed version of you.

Shunning

The ultimate, deeply tribal act of making someone invisible or 'dead to me' is an extraordinary act of violence, and for many years it was my weapon of choice. If someone let me down, betrayed me or did not live up to my expectations, then I would simply delete them from my life. Poof, dead to me. I now believe that each act of deletion has deep emotional wounding to it, and the energy spent denying the other person is denying your full potential.

Lorna Patten taught me that it's OK to bless people and let them go. She would help me to say, *'I love you, I bless you, and I release you'*. More recently, I have been exploring the power of forgiveness. Another teacher of mine, Robert Smalley, introduced me to intentional forgiveness through a series of projects and exercises, and it's changed my life.

Maybe you would like to take a vow of non-violence too.

Do no harm.

Forgive with ease.

And become a centre for love and peace for each person you meet honouring the sacred contracts of your life.

Do this, and you will be leading from the centre of the storm.

ONLINE REFERENCES

O'Neill, L. https://www.lisaoneill.co.nz

BOOKS MENTIONED

Myss, C., 2003. *Sacred Contracts: Awakening Your Divine Potential*. United States: Random House.

QUESTIONS

1 How could something undesirable you are experiencing actually be of service to you?

_____

_____

_____

2 Do you feel any obligation across your relationships? And if so what would it take to shift that away from obligation?

_____

_____

_____

3 What is your personal relationship weapon of choice? What happens when you wield that?

_____

_____

_____

4 How much love do you hold for yourself?

_____

_____

_____

5 Where in your life could forgiveness work for you?

_____

_____

_____

COMMIT TO THE COMMITTED

This chapter reminds us that not everyone wants this, or even signed up for it. Lots of people talk a good leadership, team game but don't walk it. Some people will join you, some won't, that's OK because you keep evolving for the intrinsic reward it contains. My life mantra is to follow the energy, and when a person chooses a different way, that's OK. Love them, bless them and move on.

T he leadership evolution described in this book is personal, fierce and not for everyone. Nor does it need to be. Leadership may very well be a contact sport, but it's also one of personal choice and commitment. You don't have to do anything to us as you Rise Up. You may, however, be something to those of us who choose to follow you.

I imagined a few years back what it would be like to be financially independent and retired from the need to work. Imagine through hard (smart) work and astute (consistent) investment; you had bought your time back. This exercise is less about money and more about how you might spend your time if this was true.

What would you do?

What would you say yes to?

And what would you say no to?

Would you take that meeting?

Would you continue to nurture that relationship or let it go?

Here's the thing, why wait?

I decided that even though I was not near that goal at the time, I would act as if I was. I decided to be 'that', whether I had achieved it or not. This was less a social experiment and more a decision based on living a life by design, not default. It came after observing the way people were going out at night, pretending they were networking, and then protesting that they wished to spend more time with their kids.

At the time I made this decision family was my first priority, health was my second, and committing to the committed became my filter for how I would invest the rest of my time. That, and being on my boat floating ideas around. I once owned an old 40 foot trawler for 1000 days called Sweet P, but that's a story for another time. Today as I write, meditation, contemplation and pursuit of truth take up every spare minute I have.

Get super clear about what matters most and say yes to that, politely decline the distractions of social media, television you did not choose or social obligations with no grace. We often feel chased by the things we are interested in, but spend little time on the things we are committed to.

As a result of this focus, I don't network to get ahead; I connect to inspire and be inspired. I rarely say yes to coffee catch ups and joint ventures. I don't respond to fast media requests for comment. If I am not with my family, then we had better be doing something truly worthy of the time. It's got a certain ruthless quality to it and it no doubt offends or hurts many people in my life. Any offence is not intentional; I simply don't want to waste a minute doing something that I haven't fully chosen. Lorna Patten, one of my coaches, once explained this as self-referring as opposed to self-centred – nice distinction.

Here is one of my standard responses to a request for a meeting:

Hey there,

I really appreciate you reaching out and trying to find a time to meet. Professionally, I am super focussed right now on three things: the Thought Leaders Business School, my latest book and my Conference Keynote business.

I also made a choice a few years back that I would try to have it all: family, loving relationships, deep friendships and a successful business. For this to all happen my schedule has become very compressed.

I am not taking on any new projects at this stage as I strive to deliver on my work-life integration. So I am making sure that any meetings I do have are super productive and beneficial for all parties involved.

If, knowing this, you still want to meet, then let's clarify what we can achieve together before we get together.

My business manager Sarah is the perfect person to discuss all this with, and I have CC'd her in on our conversation.

I get that this means I can't be all things to all people, but for this little duck, it's the key to focus and achieving everything I can in this busy time of life.

Thanks again for making a connection and reaching out.

Warmest Matt

Does this mean I'll miss an opportunity here or there? Absolutely, but FOMO (fear of missing out) is a concept born of lack, a scarcity idea, and one that distracts you from what you really want.

Get super clear about what matters most and say yes to that.

If you are truly at choice, what do you choose? I choose to commit to the committed. Not just those who share my blood, not just those who are in my orbit, but those who turn up to put something into life, to make a difference, shake the tree, reject the status quo. For me, that group is thought leaders – people who dare to stick their head up, have an opinion and stand for something. What do you choose? Who do you choose?

So many procrastinators will hope a relationship with you gets their job done or their goal achieved. Don't spend time feeding that fire, it doesn't help them if you do their homework. People join gyms, go to self-help seminars, and buy books without turning up to exercise, applying an idea or turning a page.

Interested is not committed.

I have learnt from years of running leadership and personal development programmes that for some people, investing in the course is the commitment. But that's like joining a gym and never actually turning up to train. The real undertaking is not the payment or enrolment in a programme; it's doing the work. When the going gets tough (and it always does), some people enrol in a new course, hopping from one programme to the next. The chart on page 215 shows you the pattern.

It's never about the money, but money is a good start. Money is the lowest form of commitment. Doing the work is what we need to stay focused on if we want to reap the rewards of our investment. The commitment ladder (see page 217) has money at the bottom, time next, then energy (the last two being the work), and finally, identity.

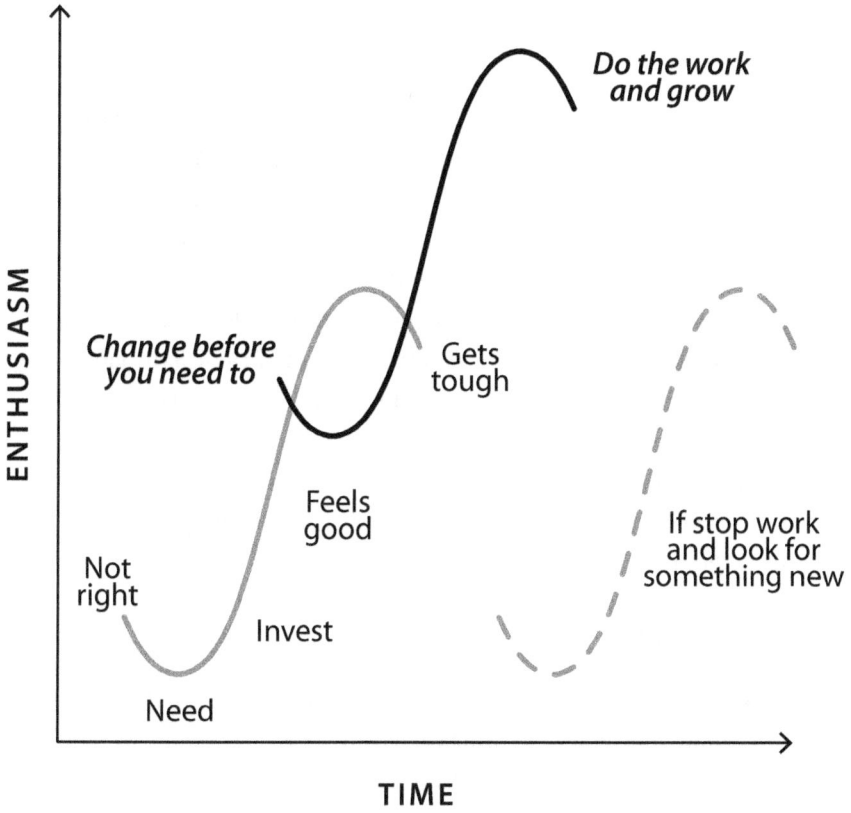

ENTHUSIASM

Do the work and grow

Change before you need to

Gets tough

Feels good

Not right

If stop work and look for something new

Invest

Need

TIME

Figure 23. **Serial commitment curve**

Thought Leaders Business School helps experts improve the financial performance of their consulting practice. Occasionally a student gets through the enrolment process with a 'This will fix it for me' mindset, when in reality only they can do the work required. You simply can't buy the result, you need to do the work. You can't outsource commitment.

You can't outsource commitment.

So what if you did not have to work, what would you do differently?

It's a great question and one that business and life coaches like to throw around with abandon. It's worth the risk of cynical disdain to ask it here, so really 'What if you did not have to work, what would you do differently?'

This question is sneaky because it's less about work and retirement or financial independence and more about life on your terms a life without compromise.

Here, then are some thoughts and suggestions around your levels of commitment to rising up.

- Be clear on what you say no to, that way you have the capacity for the things you want to say yes to. This conviction becomes a place where you can begin to live a life by design, not default.

- Get good at saying no. Commit carefully and less often.

- Don't do others' work for them, it's disempowering for them and builds resentment in you.

- Don't try to please everyone. Just accept that some will and some won't. And that what they think of you is none of your business.

- Obsess about leverage. Efficient is nice, effective is strong, but leveraged is powerful.

Identity *Character*	When it becomes who you are and what you do. You can't imagine not sticking at it.
Energy *Intensity*	Happy to be there. Putting in, getting better results than merely going through the motions.
Time *Frequency*	Sometimes turning up, putting in the time is all it takes to progress.
Money *Decision*	We know that often the 'free' is less valued. Putting skin in the game is a good start.

Figure 24. **The ladder of commitment**

- Resist the status quo. There are always likely to be faster, smarter or better way to do things than the way they've always been done.

- Get clear about what matters most to you. You only have X summers ahead of you, don't waste them in obligation, desperation or compromise.

I say no to the things that don't align, so that I can say yes to what matters. Make this your week of saying no and see what happens.

> *The real commitment is not the payment or enrolment in a programme, it's doing the work.*

My friend Rowdy McLean, author of *Play a Bigger Game*, once did a whole year of saying no. I learnt so much around this idea watching him work and live without compromise. Compassionate, considerate, generous, and focussed on making sure he did the things that mattered most, not the things we often feel obliged to do. Interestingly, he had more time for people who would not normally ask for time, and less for those he might not usually choose to help. The squeaky wheels did not get the most attention.

Counterpoint:

My biggest counterpoint to this is to be very clear that you can't be efficient with relationships. If your old dad needs to spend 10 minutes or so talking through the exhaust problem on his 1962 converted trawler (hypothetically), then it's OK. It's not about the trawler, it's about his desire to be grounded in something real. In this case to bring back to life something honest and true, rather than bob around on a show-off, plastic, mid-life crisis. It's about his desire to share that we should have a fix-it-up society, not the planned obsolescence mindset that's in most things today and leading to landfill.

Don't cut corners with the meaningful relationships in your life – they deserve genuine attention and time.

BOOKS MENTIONED

McLean, R., 2012. *Play A Bigger Game!: Achieve More! Be More! Do More! Have More!*. 1st ed. Australia: John Wiley & Sons Australia, Ltd.

QUESTIONS

1 If you did not have to work anymore, what
would you do more of in life and work?

_____

_____

_____

2 If you did not have to work anymore,
what would you do less?

_____

_____

_____

3 Is there anything you are spending a lot of
energy on right now, that you might stop
doing if you did not have to work?

_____

_____

_____

4 Is there anything you can do with that
recognition to shift the energy around it?

_____

_____

_____

5 Where in life or work could you say no more?

_____

_____

_____

AFTERWORD

Well that's it, this is my book on what I think Leadership is actually about.

If you have got this far, you realise that I believe that there is an energy behind being a leader that gets buried behind capability conversations, mission statements, spreadsheets and meetings.

I know this conversation is not for everyone. That's OK.

I know that upon reading this you may feel like you are a character in the Matrix movie, wondering whether its helpful to see the systems code or better to stay in the delusion of the illusory world.

My great hope is that this book acts not as a book full of absolute truth, but rather one with enough relative truth to help those with spirit to navigate the world they operate in.

I know in my soul that human centred leadership drives customer centred organisations that add value to the planet without negative impact.

If we can raise our consciousness as leaders the whole world benefits.

Namaste.

You've read the book.
Now see it on stage.

Matt Church understands like few others that organisations
which succeed have leaders who are inspired by what they
do and what their work stands for.

He has a rare ability to bring a room full of people along
with him for this ride. Matt's highly informative, humourous,
and energetic style saw him awarded 2014/15 Australian
Speaker of the Year, and recently named one of the Top 10
motivational speakers in the world.

So find out how he can inspire your organisation, in a theatre
before thousands or a boardroom with just your key leaders.

mattchurch.com

thOught leaders
BUSINESS
SCHOOL

Matt Church has long been passionate about helping experts deepen their thinking, broaden their reach, and increase their impact. Thought Leaders Business School is the culmination of over twenty years of his ideas and experience.

So if you've got an idea you need to share with the world Matt and the Business School team can dramatically expand your capacity to make an impact and be rewarded for it.

thoughtleaders.com.au